Sticks & Stones

BUILDING ENTREPRENEURIAL
SUCCESS FROM LIFE'S STRUGGLES

Sticks
&
Stones

NICK POWILLS

AN INC.
ORIGINAL

An Inc. Original
New York, New York
www.anincoriginal.com

Distributed by Greenleaf Book Group

For ordering information or special discounts for bulk purchases, please contact Greenleaf Book Group at PO Box 91869, Austin, TX 78709, 512.891.6100.

Design and composition by Greenleaf Book Group
Cover design by Greenleaf Book Group
Cover images used under license from ©Shutterstock.com/xpixel, ©Shutterstock.com/vilax.

Publisher's Cataloging-in-Publication data is available.

Print ISBN: 978-0-9991913-7-8

eBook ISBN: 978-0-9991913-8-5

Part of the Tree Neutral® program, which offsets the number of trees consumed in the production and printing of this book by taking proactive steps, such as planting trees in direct proportion to the number of trees used: www.treeneutral.com

Printed in the United States of America on acid-free paper

19 20 21 22 23 24 25   10 9 8 7 6 5 4 3 2 1

First Edition

This book is dedicated to my Happiness:
Sharon, Jagger, Lennon

CONTENTS

ACKNOWLEDGMENTS

After internships at *Rolling Stone* and *Details* magazines and a job as an entertainment reporter for a small daily newspaper in Chicago, I decided to make a drastic change. I joined a franchise PR firm.

A franchise PR firm was an unknown business model to me. Sure, I understood what McDonald's was, but that was the depth of my understanding. I started talking with entrepreneurs, asking them about their pathway to becoming business owners. They all had one thing in common—they had battled through adversity along the way.

Their stories were sexy to me. Some battled personal challenges, like weight or abuse. Some battled business challenges, like being told they would never go anywhere. But they were motivated.

This book is for them and the next version of them.

You are my rock stars and my business inspiration.

I wouldn't have had the fuel to accomplish greatness without a fellow kindergartner, Mike, calling me fat for the first time; my high school teacher saying I wasn't a strong writer; baseball coaches cutting me from the baseball team; my college professors thinking I wasn't responsible enough to run the school newspaper; and a boss believing my ideas were lackluster.

This book is for you. I forgive you. I also thank you for creating this burning desire for me to create something defining.

Today, that drive for success would not be where it is without the team—current and former—with whom I have had the privilege to work at No Limit Agency. Thank you to Lauren Moorman for helping edit this story so that others could be inspired.

Lastly, I must thank my people. My grandma, Mickey, who first called me an entrepreneur. My mom, Judy, and dad, Michael, for bankrolling me with pats on the back, money, and spirit. My brothers, AJ and Chris, for being rocks. And my everythings: my wife, Sharon, and sons, Jagger Wrigley and Lennon Field—my little rock stars.

The first day of kindergarten was the worst day of my life. It was the day I learned about bullying. It was the first day I was called fat.

I remember that day as if it were yesterday. My mom and I walked to school on a warm end-of-summer day. I was excited and nervous. As we approached the front entrance of Longfellow Elementary School in Oak Park, Illinois, my mom released her hand from mine. As she walked away from the biggest moment of my life at that point, another kid approached me. His name was Mike. He looked me up and down and said, "You're fat."

Time froze.

As a kid, I wasn't emotionally trained to understand what I was feeling. All I knew is how bad it felt, from my mind down to my gut and back up to my quivering lips and hot, salty tears of embarrassment. That day, I learned how a negative moment felt—and the accompanying darkness. It was branded in my memory.

When Mike, a fellow kindergartner, called me fat, he wasn't just saying, "You're fat." He was also saying, "I will make fun of you for the next twelve years—and do everything in my power to make your life a living hell."

And I let it be my hell. Until I was older, I thought about that hell every time I looked in the mirror, every time I failed, and every time I struggled with self-doubt.

For me, that day felt like the end of the world. For Mike, it was just another day. I bet he never thought about that moment again in his life.

While that impactful moment served significant negativity to me then, today, however, I understand that moment was just the beginning for me, and I've since turned one of the lowest moments of my life into fuel for what you will learn as my entrepreneurial velocity.

Everyone has defining bad moments or days. Most struggle to look at those experiences as a part of the equation—half-full versus half-empty. When you adjust your views on past struggles, the value of those moments outweighs the negative. You can then begin to leverage past struggles to accomplish anything you want.

Bullied moments will be different for everyone. For me, it was being called fat. For you, it could be being cut from a sports team, getting fired from a job, or having your parents not show pride in you. Bullied moments initially create pain in your gut and soul. For those who seek entrepreneurial velocity, those bad moments and days are temporary, a part of the equation.

For me, I used those temporary moments to build my entrepreneurial velocity to start a business. You can use the equation and entrepreneurial mindset to achieve anything. The beauty of entrepreneurial velocity is that you can take an entrepreneurial approach to your personal life and your career. Velocity ultimately comes from applying entrepreneurial attitudes and techniques to your individual life and story.

When I was called fat for the first time, it was my first true understanding of pain. I had felt pain physically (bumps and bruises) and mentally (being told no by my parents), but those are different kinds of pain. Being called fat opened up a new wound.

As a five-year-old kid, my parents had made me believe I was perfect. I didn't know I was capable of having a flaw. Learning that I did, the way I did, was pretty painful. It turned my happy-go-lucky, glass-half-full childhood upside down.

We've all had to overcome obstacles. You can probably remember a moment like mine, crystal clear. You might also remember understanding what being bullied felt like.

I no longer look back on these moments and feel bad. I use them as fuel. It's all part of the plan.

Because I was teased for being fat when I was a kid, I am now more health-conscious, which impacts my body and soul on a daily basis.

In high school, I was told I wasn't a good enough writer to work on the student newspaper. I now own a communications agency and two publications. Turns out, my teachers, my bosses, and my bullies were wrong.

In college, I was the only editor-in-chief of the student newspaper to not have a faculty advisor—because they said I was being too creative with my ideas. Look where creativity got me today, starting and running two businesses, both of which have challenged the norm for the way brands can communicate to their targets (more on that later).

In life, many painful moments may become forever etched in your mind. They will torture you, shape you, and define you. For me those moments fueled my ability to be an open book with my employees; to be confident in communicating with my significant other; to be confident when speaking in front of a giant audience; to be comfortable in telling my life story, with the hope of being able to help others who have gone through tough and memorable moments.

Understanding your moments of fuel—perceived negative events that will later turn into fuel for whatever you are trying to accomplish—will be essential to preparing for your success.

Whether setting out to achieve a personal goal or deciding to create your business, or both, start by addressing the challenges you have faced and how you have overcome them. Be vulnerable with your past; it will help you shape your plan. Think back as far as you can about all the times you've been told no. What moments stick out as challenges? At what points did you feel your world was collapsing? In retrospect, aren't those moments now motivating? Do they motivate you to do something brilliant? Think about how you could have leveraged those fights, struggles, and challenges differently.

When reflecting on my path, I now understand how each moment of my life established my foundation for accomplishing something wonderful. I understand how I used those moments, experiences, and struggles to create my entrepreneurial velocity—a place where brick walls are shattered, challenges are accompanied by solutions, and confidence in everything I do is at an all-time high. Each step of my life has contributed to the equation.

Understanding the velocity equation will be essential for you in identifying the perceived negative moments that have led you to this point. What is your fat moment?

To get to velocity, you will need foundation and momentum. Your foundation is made up of your fuel (failures, challenges, bullied moments, and stalled ventures); your people (your rocks, your support systems); and your belief that anything is possible.

FOUNDATION = FUEL + PEOPLE + BELIEF

Your momentum starts the second you stop seeing the cup as half-empty instead of half-full. You certainly don't forget those hurtful moments, but you can forgive others for them and start believing in yourself.

MOMENTUM = CONFIDENCE + ONE INCH OF DIFFERENCE + INITIAL PARTS OF ACTION

Your entrepreneurial velocity is the moment when brick walls no longer exist. Velocity comes from your life experiences plus your career experiences plus your personal drive and missions. Velocity and the leverage of fuel is vital to long-term success, as it gives you the ability to believe that anything is possible and the strength to bust through any brick wall you face.

FOUNDATION + MOMENTUM = VELOCITY

Anyone who has experienced bullying or failure that has led to self-doubt or stagnation can benefit from reflection and understanding. The decision to make a change in your life or start a business will initially be a tough decision. But ultimately, you either do it or you don't. Maybes exist, but they are the easy way out.

For humans, the first step is not easy—you know, the one where you decide to make a change, take a risk for the chance to change your life's path. When I decided to start losing weight, it wasn't a decision made overnight. It was a decision that took years of walking up to the starting line and turning around. It took finding the value of the first time being called fat. Same for starting a business. It took much reflection, planning, and trial before I decided to change my career and become an entrepreneur.

My plan for this book is to provide you with stories, sadness, laughter, and success. I want to share with you my foundation, my momentum, and my entrepreneurial velocity to help you jump-start whatever you're looking to accomplish: losing weight, starting a business, running a mile, or writing a book.

My goal for this book is to provide you with a blueprint to discover your own foundation + momentum = velocity, setting you on a path to create whatever you dream of.

I want you to believe in the seemingly impossible. I want my experience to teach you that we all have gone through hard times, and I want my words to show you how to overcome them.

I want you to think deeply about your foundation and your momentum and how they will ultimately guide you to your personal velocity. I will show you the power of transforming your pain into fuel. I will also teach those who are the future entrepreneurs of this world that the challenges you go through in the early part of your life will make you better. If you stay committed through the roadblocks of life and business, happiness is ultimately achievable.

What you must understand, as an entrepreneur or for personal gain, is that success does not happen easily—nor do dreams magically come true. Achievement comes with hard work, vision, and execution.

When it comes to planning your entrepreneurial journey or strengthening your personal journey, you must create a plan that is built around great people, a solid selling strategy, and, ultimately, profits. No matter where you are in your journey—whether you are ready to become an entrepreneur tomorrow or still need ten more years—make each moment count and consider them wins in your greater plan.

As we move forward, I am going to share with you my plans, including the one that led me to becoming self-employed, achieving my vision of becoming an entrepreneur.

In the following pages, you'll learn that it is easy to figure out your path to success as long as you are ready to reflect on your past to bump you to the future. To accomplish something great, you don't have to start at zero.

This book is for the stalled-out employee who still has a glimmer of hope for the top, the entrepreneur who is ready to start a business and is afraid of the unsupported unknown, and anyone who is ready to stop using life obstacles as excuses.

When deciding you are ready to own your own success, you will find that your personal and business lives will mix well together. The fuel from your personal life and the fire to achieve a life that is better will help prepare you for what's next in your story, one that you author and narrate.

Oftentimes it takes hitting rock bottom to realize that your personal decisions directly impacted your outcomes. In life, there are those things you can control (e.g., what you put into your body) and those that you can't (e.g., the airplane you fly in when traveling). It is up to you to take responsibility for the things you can control and not sweat the stuff you can't.

The good news is that velocity will be judged on a curve—and you own the curve. You decide when you make it—when you figure out what makes happiness, what I refer to throughout the book as =happiness. =Happiness is the moment you can bask in your success, even if just for a moment. =Happiness is what we are all striving for and, frankly, can all accomplish. =Happiness should equal your velocity.

If you are willing to adjust, lean on others, and listen to what you learn through your experiences, you should be able to set yourself up for the greatest chance at winning and, in turn, achieving =happiness.

PART 1

Foundation

When I was five, my grandmother called me an entrepreneur for the first time. I felt deflated that day.

I had just sold her my first book, a word-for-word copy of *Go, Dog. Go!* Naturally—to her, at least—calling me her little entrepreneur made sense. She was showing me love and affection, belief and possibility. However, for a kid who was being bullied and called fat, this new word had another meaning. My perception was that it was another incident of name-calling.

"I hate you, Grandma," I replied.

With no understanding of what the word meant as a five-year-old "entrepreneur," I figured it was another word for failure, misshapen, or loser, so I jumped the gun in my rebuttal. Boy, was my perception off.

"Nick, it's a good thing," she said, calming my fear that this was bad. "It means that you have a lot of creative energy to fulfill your great ideas."

This moment of support was another piece of my foundation— a critical one. It was the moment that would forever stick in my memory. It was a moment of belief.

You probably have your own memories of similar situations too. Those memories will be important to your foundation.

Your foundation is composed of your fuel, your people, and your belief. This is the foundational equation essential to whatever you plan to accomplish:

FUEL + PEOPLE + YOUR BELIEF = YOUR FOUNDATION.

Fuel

Fuel comes from recognizing moments of the past as drivers, not detractors. In the moment, I felt poorly when called fat for the first time. While it still hurts, it now acts as a driver and motivates me to accomplish something great.

When identifying fuel for your foundation, you will need to start recognizing negative moments as a part of your story. You will need to understand the moments that were turbulent but necessary for constructing your drive.

Negative perceptions can be a risk for never establishing a foundation. If I had always seen being called fat as a negative, I would have never established that moment as a part of my foundation.

However, fuel can come from almost any moment that challenges you. While it may be first perceived as a negative moment or a loss, all negatives and losses with a flipped perception can turn into positives and wins. Being cut from a team, being told you are not creative enough, or being told your idea will never work may suck in the moment, but these moments can be turned into fuel for your foundation if you perceive the challenge differently.

In the moment, sometimes we don't realize the teaching value of a negative experience because the emotional pain is greater than the potential positive outcome. Once you begin to believe that you can overcome tough moments, you can start using them as fuel for your foundation. If you view the tough moments as negatives, they will cause a downward spiral into dissatisfaction, fear, and a lack of accomplishment—a deterrent to success.

How do you turn these moments? How do you change your perceptions of a half-empty experience into a half-full experience? Partly through maturing and life experiences. Partly through making a conscious decision to view the experience as a learning lesson.

As a child, it would be nearly impossible for me to change my perception of that moment of being called fat, as I didn't have enough life experiences to teach me how. At that point, bad felt bad; I saw situations in black and white. Later in life, my experiences helped support a different view of the negative experience. This is where experiences helped turn half-empty moments into half-full moments. Whereas, when called an entrepreneur, I was able to quickly gain clarity about that being a good thing. As I have gotten older, it's much easier to minimize the pain of the fat moment and recognize it as a part of my fuel.

It's interesting to talk about this with fellow entrepreneurs and people who have accomplished something great. When I describe the parts of the entrepreneurial velocity equation, they instantly connect. They tell stories about being bullied, abused, losing, or told no. They talk about how remembering these moments has created an energy in them to create something great. They are out to prove disbelievers wrong. The fascinating thing about the grandma moment is that it could have been another bullied moment saved in my fuel bank had I not understood that it was actually positive. My grandma moment is the second part of the equation—people—as well as the third part, belief.

As you continue to reflect on your own experiences, you will start to see bridges to different parts of the equation in singular moments.

Fuel, as you reflect, will be important. Chances are, it will be fairly easy for you to come by. You are probably identifying with your own "fat" moment right now.

EXERCISE

Write down a painful experience (e.g., the first time being called fat).

People

People is the next piece of your foundation. People are those who support you: your grandmother who calls you an entrepreneur; your teacher who believes you have the potential to create something great; your family, who supports you in your dream to accomplish something big. People will help build your foundation. When mixed with fuel, their praises become even more powerful.

When it comes to finding your people, whether at age five or fifty, finding your rocks, your believers (people who always have your back), is critical.

Rocks come in various shapes and sizes. Some entrepreneurs will say they fought their mentor/rock until the mentor admitted how proud they were of the entrepreneur. Some rocks provide unconditional love, like a parent. Some rocks don't buy into all of your ideas one-hundred-percent. Rather they challenge and push you to come up with a better answer.

When my grandmother called me an entrepreneur, she was simply saying that she believed in me, that she was my cheerleader. While she was standing up and establishing herself as one of my rocks—my people—she was also putting a little belief in my foundation. In order for you to pull the belief out of people, you have to believe that what they are telling you is valuable to your mission. She was showing that she was a rock and a believer. She saw something in the five-year-old version of me that she wanted to call out as having potential. She put on the "Nick's No. 1" foam finger and waved it high in the air.

She was the people ingredient of my foundation recipe.

EXERCISE

Write down a list of people who have supported you. Start with five (e.g., parents, grandmother, spouse):

1.

2.

3.

4.

5.

Belief

Your belief is a natural progression from your fuel and your people. It is the moment when you start to build your own confidence. You start to believe that you can accomplish what you are setting out to win at. When you believe anything is possible, you have the support and you have fuel moments to create your vision and, ultimately, build your foundation.

My grandma calling me an entrepreneur was her being my rock. Me embracing the fact that maybe this was a point of differentiation for me and my story was me having belief in myself.

Write down three situations where you have shown confidence (e.g., two of mine were starting my own business and copying word-for-word *Go, Dog. Go!*):

1.

2.

3.

EXERCISE

Foundation

Your foundation is your story. What you do with it is your formula.

The truth is, whether you have recognized it or not, you have all the ingredients of the foundation. You have a story that has led you up to this point. You have pain points, rocks, and the ability to identify belief that you can create something amazing.

By this point, you are starting to think about transforming your moments—the good, bad, and ugly—into fuel for your ultimate vision (the big thing you want to accomplish).

Your vision is your goal. For me, I ended up using my formula to create No Limit Agency, the business that motivated me to quit my job and go out on my own. For you, it could be as simple as getting into business for yourself. It could even be accomplishing something personally. I have used the same equation to help me run my first half marathon and to make adjustments in my diet.

The beauty of the equation is that once you master your version, you can apply it to other visions over and over again.

CHAPTER 1

Fuel

During the summer of 2000, after my freshman year of college, I worked a summer internship at the *Wednesday Journal*, a small community newspaper in Oak Park, Illinois. I earned this internship through the parts of foundation: I was told I couldn't write; I pushed for an opportunity and gained people support; and I then believed that I could accomplish great things. My vision was to become a great writer.

My internship was to cover local sports and write a bowling column, and in exchange I received summer press passes to the Chicago Cubs and White Sox.

Halfway through the summer, I was working on a story about athletes remembering their childhood—what it was like to dream about playing professional baseball and accomplish it. I had compiled interviews with some of the league's greatest athletes—future Hall of Famers Frank Thomas, Derek Jeter, and Ken Griffey Jr.

I then set out to interview one of my favorites growing up, Will Clark, who played primarily for the San Francisco Giants in the late eighties through the early nineties.

When I played pickup baseball in front of my house as a youngster, I would pretend I was Frank Thomas, Mark Grace, or Will Clark. Clark was a sports hero to me and someone I aspired to be like when I grew up.

Per usual that summer, I took the Red Line to Wrigley Field, walked the short block to the field, gained my press access, and walked down the stairway onto the perfect grass and dirt.

That year, the Cardinals had signed Clark to fill in for regular first baseman Mark McGwire, who was battling injuries. I wanted him to be the final piece to my story.

I walked through the dugout, into the visitors' locker room, and immediately recognized Mr. Will Clark. I took a deep breath, as I usually did to calm my nerves before meeting my heroes, and walked up to him. What happened next was nothing a deep breath could have prepared me for.

Just like with the other larger-than-life athletes, I asked if I could ask him a few questions.

"Who the fuck are you?" he said with a half smile.

I figured he was just messing around with me. "I am Nick Powills, and I work with the *Wednesday Journal*. I am working on—"

"The Wednesday fucking what?" he shouted back. "You didn't say the *Chicago Tribune*, did you?"

"No, sir, it's a weekly newspaper out of Oak—"

This continued for what felt like an eternity but, in reality, was probably only a few short minutes.

As I walked away—red faced and deeply disappointed—I noticed out of the corner of my eye a guy laughing at me.

Great. Another bully, I thought.

As I walked near him on my way out of the locker room, he said, "Wow, that was tough. Are you walking up to the press box?"

I replied yes, and he said he would accompany me. As we walked to the Wrigley Field press box, he reminded me that those moments happen to the best of us and that I would eventually reflect on this moment and laugh about it.

We ended up talking throughout the whole game about baseball and, at that time, the Cubs' misery. Not once did I ask who he was. I only knew him as Rich. He told me he was writing a story about remembering the Cubs and the grit that came along with being a fan. I was flattered. A real writer was talking to a dreamer.

As the ninth inning wrapped up and the Cubs racked up another loss, the guy handed me a piece of paper with his name and phone number. He then said, "Congratulations, Nick. You just landed yourself on the top of the intern list at *Rolling Stone* magazine. I am Rich Cohen, an editor, and I would love to have you as an intern next summer."

I was in disbelief that a moment so rough could turn so magical.

He also wrote about the Will Clark moment in a *Harper's Bazaar* article, "Down and Out at Wrigley Field: A Prayer for the Chicago Cubs," in August of 2001. In this moment, I found fuel in Will Clark screaming at me; I found a rock in Rich Cohen seeing my potential; and I was able to take both and turn them into belief that maybe, just maybe, I was a good enough interviewer, storyteller, conversationalist, and writer to accomplish something amazing. In this moment, Rich was instrumental to helping me turn a bullied moment into fuel, too. He helped me see how to laugh about it and told me that one day I would look back on the moment and see it differently.

From that experience, I learned that everything happens for a reason and the happenings that don't kill you have the opportunity to morph into fuel for your foundation. Bad things happen all the time. But when they happen to good people, hopefully a better moment is waiting for them at the next turn.

For me, bad days began with the first day of being called fat. Your bad days probably follow a similar path, beginning with a bad moment in time.

I didn't know being called an entrepreneur for the first time would stick with me for as long as it has. I didn't know being yelled at by one of my favorite players would have such great power.

Bullies are only bullies if you let them be. But bullies can be useful. If you are willing to view their torment in a new way, you can turn it into fuel that will propel you into doing something great.

You, too, have a Will Clark in your back pocket. It's just a matter of remembering, pulling it out, understanding the value of the moment, and using it to jump-start anything blocking the execution of whatever great thing you want to accomplish.

Take a second and think about the last bad day you had. Did you have a fight with your significant other, an encounter with your jerk of a boss, or worse?

Maybe you came home from work frustrated because expectations of you were too high and you struggled to meet them. Your initial reaction was likely negative, and there's nothing wrong with that; that's how most people behave. But if you remained negative about it, it would be hard to use it as motivation to destroy the expectations next time.

Take a step back and reflect on what you could have done differently. Was not meeting expectations a matter of effort, attention, or both? Did you have a chance to succeed? Did you communicate properly or challenge the communication to better understand the ask?

In many cases, especially when it comes to bad moments you can have some control over, you can step out of your shoes and try to find some things you would have done differently.

The easiest way to flip this perception is to apply it to your vision. Say to yourself that you are going to learn as much as you possibly can. If you frame it this way, that moment becomes fuel instead of being a negative. That moment, whether it sticks in your memory forever or not, will ultimately help lead you to whatever you are trying to accomplish, no matter how small or how big.

There will be and have been good people and bad people in your life. There are those who tell you no many more times than yes, and they often say no for the sake of saying no. Sure, your people will sometimes challenge you to a better outcome, but nos without a chance are brutal. There are those who make it hard to believe that you can accomplish greatness. No, you will not be a great baseball player. No, you will not be a great writer. No, you are not good-looking. No, you will not be a great business partner. All of those nos bottled up equal more nos. And that sucks.

When someone tells you no simply because they can or because they would like to overpower you, these are nos of power.

A no is when you feel in your heart that you could win at something, but someone tells you no. A yes in your life is when someone gives you a chance and tells you they believe in you.

All the hundred thousand nos I've been given have aided me in the search for perfection—graded on a curve, of course. Those nos are my fuel to find more yeses and to be the most successful person I can be in my career, in my family, and in my life.

The yeses will also be fuel and will come from the people who support you. Yeses will help you build on your fuel. They will lead you to finding great rocks/believers and will push you to believe in yourself.

To start using the pieces of your story to build your foundation, work through this exercise. Look back at moments in your life and identify those that serve as the fuel (perceived negative moments changed to being perceived as positive) ingredient in your foundational recipe:

Tough moment(s) in your life:

How you felt:

How it impacts you today:

How you have overcome those challenges:

How you will continue to overcome those challenges:

What you wish you could have done differently to adjust that experience:

What you will do from this day on to improve the foundation of the experience:

How your personal situation impacts your business momentum:

What your eventual success (your end goal completed) looks like:

Whether you are a former fatty, a former high school baseball team failure, or a dismissed writer, look back and change your view of that moment to be fuel. Leverage it to look forward. In life, that's the only direction we should look toward. Learn from the past but be willing to turn over a new leaf every day.

CHAPTER 2

People

People are essential to the foundational equation. Imagine how fuel would work without them. People are the important secret sauce. How your people support you and support your vision will ultimately dictate what happens to your goals and dreams. People are that essential to success.

You will need to find people—your rocks—who will support and cheerlead your vision. If they don't, your vision for creating something amazing will never have a chance to turn from foundation to momentum to velocity.

Had my foundation not been as sound as it was with the people ingredient, who knows what decisions I would have made? Unconditional love and emotional support will be important to have regardless of the situation. This is a part of the people stage in the equation, and you will see people fit into your foundation in a few ways.

You will turn to them as your motivation for building more strength to accomplish greatness (becoming healthier for your children, earning more money for your family, having greater impact on your community) and you will call on them for support (making you feel good about the steps you are taking to accomplish something great).

You will lean on them as a shoulder, a sounding board, to help you stand back up when tough moments happen alongside you creating your vision.

The first day I was called fat, what would have happened if my mom wasn't there to comfort me? The first day I was cut from the baseball team, what would have happened if my dad wasn't there to tell me it's the team's loss? The first time I was rejected from a writing job, what would have happened if someone at the school didn't explore my potential and give me a chance? The first time an employer told me I wasn't good enough, what would have happened if there wasn't another leader encouraging me to keep trying? The first time I was told my business idea was bad, what would have happened if a friend wasn't there to tell me they were wrong?

Your people will give you different types of support. Sometimes they will pat you on the back for accomplishing something great, and sometimes they will simply give you encouragement.

There is tremendous reward from receiving both types of praise. The praise serves as motivators. When someone tells you how great you are, you might feel goosebumps go down your back. Along the way, when you are establishing your pathway for creating something amazing, those pats on the back will fuel you to want more. They will become addictive. They will encourage you to keep fighting to establish your foundation, your momentum, and your velocity.

What you will recognize as you continue to build upon your own story and equation is that the equation will have shifts. I still have fuel moments—a client firing us, an employee quitting. You will probably see this too. As you reflect, some people may support parts of your equation, but not all. For me, teachers have offered support when I was battling through some trying moments and struggling to see my visions through; however, these teachers are no longer in the picture. This is OK.

Just having enough good people around at all points will help you identify this part of the foundation equation.

In order to eventually lose weight, I needed my wife and my sons to love me unconditionally before I could envision a long, healthy life. I needed other people to say, "It looks like you lost a lot of weight" or "You look great."

In business, I needed my clients to tell me I had a special idea, my parents to cheerlead the idea of quitting my job and moving to Atlanta, my girlfriend-turned-wife to listen to my wins and losses every day, and my friends to take an active interest in the business.

People, neighbors, community, friends—they're all vital to your path of success.

My parents, Mike and Judy, encouraged my dreams. Never once did they tell fat Nick that he would never become a baseball player. In fact, if I told my dad today that I was quitting my job to try to become a ball player, he would probably support it. They have my back.

My wife, Sharon, encourages me on a daily basis to build something special. She has my back. My children, Jagger and Lennon, give me hugs and kisses when I get home from a long day. They have my back.

My friends Sean and Steve help me work through business challenges on a daily basis, providing advice, guidance, and support.

My great clients cheerlead the successes of our agency and business by telling others they love working with us.

My team at my office put in their best efforts each day on a mission to build the brands we work with. Without great people, the agency I have built, No Limit Agency, could never have become a great agency. Greatness will be impossible without great people.

Who are your current people? Who do you perceive to support your every step, unconditionally, to give you a shoulder when you need it, a hand when you want it, and sometimes, even access to their pocketbooks to keep your idea afloat?

EXERCISE

Make a list of five people who support you:

1.

2.

3.

4.

5.

At this point, you have begun to think about your fuel moments and the people who support you. Are you starting to believe you can accomplish your next great event more? Are you connecting the fuel and people dots and realizing the value of each?

Good.

Now comes your belief.

CHAPTER 3

Belief

I n the final part of the foundation equation, you must establish your belief. You must believe—truly believe—that you have the ability and the power to eventually accomplish your vision.

Belief is the most important ingredient of your foundation. Without it, you will not be able to leverage your fuel and people to accomplish your vision. The biggest difference between those who accomplish greatness and those who don't is that those who win believe they can.

Belief comes from inside. It's yours. It is established through your story. It is your grit, your attitude, and your hustle. All of which will lead you to have a desire to create something amazing.

Grit is the strength of your character. It is built from your fuel moments.

Attitude is your approach. It is seeing opportunities as half-full. It is approaching your goals with an anything-is-possible attitude.

Hustle is your ability to work harder than anyone else. It is running one more lap or making one more sales call.

The combination of the three components will lead to your belief. Belief is built from grit, attitude, and hustle, which, in turn, becomes confidence. Belief happens when you bottle up your tough fuel moments and apply them to increasing the strength of your confidence. For many, confidence is not something they were born with; it is something they had to earn. The strength of your confidence comes from building on each winning moment. The more you try and succeed, the more confident you get.

With any failure or struggle (for me it was being the fat kid), it's hard to find belief in the ability to disrupt. Failure sucks, but as we discussed earlier, it can be leveraged into fuel and ultimately confidence. Confidence is built from your life story and your experiences. If you are told you are the best athlete and the smartest person and the best looking from your first days of understanding language and people, you will probably have a much easier time accessing your place of confidence, but you will also have to dig deeper to find your fuel. If you are the fat kid, good luck, as you are going to have to disrupt your personal norm to believe in the possible. But once you start believing, that sudden turn can be monumental to placing you on a journey toward strength. You will decide to hustle. You will do so with an attitude. You will battle adversity with grit. You will learn to believe in yourself and begin to dream big.

Dreamers who turn their dreams into realities are ultimately the most successful people in this world. Those that don't let a no get in their way live life accomplishing exactly what they want to accomplish. Dreamers certainly run into obstacles. While they don't run through brick walls quite yet, they start to showcase belief by bouncing back from challenges they face.

For me, the combination of events in my life before No Limit Agency helped to establish my belief. If any of those pieces of my foundation did not happen the way they did, I am not sure I would be in the same place I am in today. Embracing your failures and successes is how you reframe a half-empty cup to be a half-full cup.

Michael Jordan once said, "I have missed more than nine thousand shots in my career. I have lost almost three hundred games. On twenty-six occasions, I have been entrusted to take the game-winning shot, and I missed. I have failed over and over and over again in my life. And that is why I succeed."

He certainly was someone who could find success in failure. His X factor was grit, attitude, and hustle—the will to never, ever give up. Whether making a team or winning a game, his fuel, people, and belief are apparent in much of the greatness he achieved.

He was cut from the high school team, yet he went on to be arguably the greatest athlete that ever lived—and he will proudly tell you that he is.

He isn't alone in the idea that great leaders and success stories are born from failure.

Albert Einstein didn't learn to speak until he was four or read until he was seven.

Walt Disney was fired from his newspaper job for lacking imagination and good ideas.

The Beatles were told by a record company that they didn't like their sound.

Thomas Edison failed a thousand times at creating the lightbulb before figuring out the solution.

Would you call any of the above failures? Of course not. They built grit from these moments, had a positive attitude, and worked their butts off to accomplish greatness. They had to take the fuel moment and use it to motivate their drive for their vision.

As you can see with the Michael Jordan example, grit (built from him getting cut), attitude (knowing he was better than others gave him credit for), and hustle (stopping at nothing to prove others wrong) should all be character traits seen in any successful moment you have or will accomplish.

Grit is a characteristic that will help you battle through the foundation part of the equation. Grit should be a result of your fuel.

For me, I can see grit, attitude, and hustle when I was trying to become a writer at my high school newspaper. After getting cut from the high school baseball team (no, I did not have the skills of Michael Jordan to prove the coaches wrong), I decided to focus on becoming a sports writer. However, the teacher lead of the school newspaper at Oak Park River Forest High School told me my writing wasn't good enough to become a sports writer for the paper. Similar to Jordan, as a junior in high school, I took things into my own hands.

I emailed (using AOL—at the time, the most popular Internet provider) a columnist at the *Chicago Tribune*, Fred Mitchell (he also had AOL and provided his email address at the end of his column), asking for advice on how to become a great writer like him. We exchanged a few emails, and then I pushed. I leveraged my grit: "Fred, is there any chance I could shadow you while you cover the Chicago Bears' home games?"

He must have seen something in me that the high school teacher couldn't because he invited me to come to the next home game and accompany him in the press box to learn the art of sports writing.

Skeptical that a *Chicago Tribune* columnist would welcome me as his apprentice/intern simply through an email exchange, my dad, to ensure my safety, dropped me off at Soldier Field.

In the first game I covered, the Bears were playing the New York Jets. It was November 16, 1997. There I was, someone not good enough to write but good enough to talk another writer into teaching him, sitting in a press box, rubbing shoulders with the biggest sports writers in Chicago. I was ready to work through my first story.

Throughout the game, I took notes on the progression. Fred explained that when you write, you cannot be a fan. You have to tell the story in an unbiased way. After the game, he said it was up to me to get great quotes from the players and coaches to support the story.

I walked down the ramps to the press conference room. Bill Parcells was the head coach of the Jets. Known as being a rough, tough coach, he barreled into the room. As he busted into the tight visitors' press conference room, he angrily bumped me, and I, my backpack, and my tape recorder fell to the ground. He quickly bent down, helped me to my feet, whispered asking if I was OK, and then continued to showcase his distaste for the media.

The Bears had lost the game 23–15 and were not in the best of moods, but that wasn't going to stop me from getting great quotes. I asked a question to head coach Dave Wannstedt. I asked a few questions and got an autograph (and later learned asking for autographs is a journalistic no-no) from Rashaan Salaam, Chris Zorich, and Curtis Conway. I was on fire.

I returned back to the press box and wrote my story alongside Fred, who had a deadline to hit. I watched, learned, and pushed myself.

That night, I logged onto AOL and emailed Fred my story. He sent back some edits, and I finalized my first sports story. The story was never published but the experience was great practice.

Fred—like my mom, my grandma, my dad—was another one of my people. It's essential you find similar supporters along your way, even those who only enter for a short period of time. Today, Fred is not in my life, but he remains an integral part of my equation.

This process with Fred continued a few more times. I then returned to the teacher who told me I wasn't good enough to work on the school newspaper, and I handed him my portfolio of Bears stories. He asked how I worked my way into the locker room. I told my story. He listened. We negotiated, and he put me on the school newspaper (more on that later).

Grit, attitude, and hustle helped me win that first writing opportunity. Grit in that I had been told I wasn't a good enough writer to write for the school paper, but I was willing to fight for my chance to prove that I was. Attitude in that I was willing to listen to any and all advice on how to make my storytelling stronger. Hustle in that I was willing to do whatever it took to be given a chance. I bet you have a story that showcases all three components.

When creating my visions—losing weight or starting businesses and being a successful entrepreneur—I've never experienced an overnight success. Currently, I am certainly not considered great or legendary in my field, yet I embrace my failures as another step toward success. I embrace the need to fail in order to build a foundation that can create momentum that can turn into entrepreneurial velocity. Eventually, I tell myself, I will be the greatest my industry (PR, franchising) has ever seen.

What moments can you recall when you believed anything was possible? What moments did you push through failure and use it as leverage? What moments did you dream and accomplish? Take a minute to reflect on these and enjoy the wins of your past. If you are an entrepreneur working your way through the momentum stage or someone still trying to find their way in their career, their life, their marriage, or their business, reflecting on the stories of the past is an essential piece to finding your entrepreneurial or personal velocity. The past will fuel your future.

Write down three personal- or business-related grit, attitude, and hustle moments in your life that at the time seemed like a failure or a miss but now, when added up, make sense as a part of what you have become today and in your belief that you can accomplish something amazing:

Continued

EXERCISE

Grit

   1.

   2.

   3.

Attitude

   1.

   2.

   3.

Hustle

   1.

   2.

   3.

As you reflect, you will start to find your belief from your fuel and then from the people supporting you. When nos come your way—especially those that come your way without data and from nonbelievers—you will hear them, but you will not listen to them. You will understand your grit, attitude, and hustle. And you'll begin to pull these pieces together to help you find motivation to accomplish your vision.

While in the foundation stage, don't forget that there may be turbulence. You will gain wins, but sometimes those wins will face additional bumps.

After reviewing the stories that I wrote with Fred Mitchell, the teacher said, "I am sorry, but there really isn't a position for you on the school newspaper for next year."

Nos can derail your idea—however, when you start understanding your own grit, attitude, and hustle, you can start to turn the nos into fuel. When my teacher told me no, without data, I heard him, but I didn't listen.

"It really is my dream to become a journalist. Is there anything I can do to join the staff? Even if you don't let me write, I will do anything."

He listened to my negotiation and offered an alternative—saying that if I went to summer journalism camp, he would give me a shot on the school newspaper for my senior year.

The next time someone tells you that you failed, or you know you made a mistake, look at it as a stepping stone to success. You decide if you want to listen to that no or do something with it. That half-full approach will help fuel you to finding your purpose.

Don't ever let someone tell you that you can't do something. The person who told Jordan he couldn't make the team, told Einstein he was dumb for not being able to read, told Disney he wasn't creative, or told Nick Powills he couldn't write was wrong. Perhaps, in those moments, the foundation for each story wasn't established; thus, greatness wasn't seen yet. Perhaps without those nos, greatness wouldn't have started.

I bet, though, if those who said no had had a better understanding of the impact of those moments and the pain they created, they may have changed their approach. You should think about this too. How can you motivate others without immediate, dataless nos? How can you use positivity to encourage others—the same way you want others to encourage you?

In both life and in business, I have learned the value of positive thinking and believe in its potential to spread. Whether pitching the media a story I believe should be on the front page of their newspaper, believing that I can avoid the bread at the dinner table and ultimately remove it from my diet forever, or believing that my agency will be the best fit for a potential client—all beliefs are built from the mentality that anything is possible.

Leverage your understanding of stepping stones to further establish your belief in your vision. Ideas are just ideas unless you execute and truly believe that anything is possible.

EXERCISE

Write down a challenging moment you've experienced.

Draw a line and connect it to a moment when you felt great about whatever dream you were trying to achieve. How did that experience influence the possibility of momentum in your moment?

Now, establish your vision. For you, what does success look like? Is it money, fame, happiness? Write down your answer.

Now, visualize how you feel within that vision, what you look like, and what that winning formula looks like. Think about it for a minute. Hold on to that image, as it will be important to planning for your winning moment and learning to believe that anything is possible.

CHAPTER 4

Starting Your Vision and the Pathway to Momentum

I am not a billionaire entrepreneur. I am simply on a planned path of success. I am realistic about the baby steps needed to build the foundation to gain some momentum and have a shot at velocity. I care deeply about the path and journey it takes to win.

With a foundation established, your next step is to create your vision and define your blueprint. The establishment of your vision is the gateway to momentum. Your foundation will have value because you have recognized your fuel, people, and belief, but without a vision, you won't be able to leverage it.

What does success look like? What do you want to accomplish?

Take a moment and think about where you are right now. Have you begun to think about your personal journeys and your future dreams? What do you want to ultimately accomplish? Have you thought about your own fuel and the people who will support you? Have you thought about your current belief in what you want to accomplish and how you are going to access hustle, attitude, and grit from your life to boost your confidence?

EXERCISE

Work through the following exercise so that you can start identifying your own vision.

If I could change one thing about myself, it would be:

If I could change one thing about my business/career, it would be:

How can I change one thing about myself?

How can I change one thing about my business/career?

What three goals do I wish to accomplish over the next three months?

How will I feel if those goals are not hit?

ARE YOU READY?

Whether losing weight or starting a business, understanding the foundational structure of the velocity equation has been essential to me finding success. The structure is not bulletproof. Bumps and bruises will continue to happen—that's a part of life—but it can be applied to anything you want to accomplish.

When planning to jump off the ledge to accomplish something big and go after your vision, you are faced with the tough decision of whether you should do it or not. Can you sidestep excuses and make a giant change in your life? If the answer is no for now, then embrace that moment, go back to the drawing board, continue your planning, and step back from the ledge. Eventually, when you allow yourself to understand how to leverage the fuel that you have earned, the people who back you, and the belief built from your life's experiences, you will be led to the opportunity to create greatness. For this to happen you need a proper vision.

Take your fuel, people, and belief and cross-apply them to your next vision. To help build your plan with your foundational equation, we are going to work through your formula. I will show you an example of mine, from 2008:

What is the business I want to create or goal I want to accomplish? No Limit Media Consulting, a social media/public relations boutique communications agency.

Why am I creating this?

I gave my boss a hundred-page business plan on how to transform his agency into a social media agency, too. He said social media was a fad. I see an opportunity to create something bigger. My mission statement is (written in 2007):

No Limit Media Consulting, a full-service communications agency dedicated to providing the franchise industry with more than just the basics of public relations, extends the boundaries of limited client relationships through marketing and hands-on strategic growth campaigns. By becoming ingrained in the growth of companies small and large, No Limit Media Consulting differentiates itself from the typical public relations firms by acting as a valuable part of the company rather than just a supplier. It offers traditional PR with a robust digital strategy that includes social media.

In the franchise industry, current public relations firms box the client in by placing a limit on the services they receive. The firms don't further educate themselves so that they can extend their services and truly earn the retainers they charge. No Limit Media Consulting takes client satisfaction to the next level by building more centralized relationships with strong staff support systems and the desire to go the extra mile for each and every client.

No Limit Media Consulting is enthusiastic about helping companies grow by offering not only the media support—both traditional and social—but also the critical consulting to achieve the growth goals and brand the company right.

What do I expect to happen?

No Limit Media Consulting will start recruiting clients that want more than just PR—more of a full strategy to put their messages in front of the right audiences.

What experiences in my past have helped me prepare to start this (fuel)?

The first day I was called fat still sticks with me. Teachers and bosses not believing I can become a great writer/communicator and drive business. My boss telling me that social media is a fad. My boss not giving me a chance to grow his business with him.

What have been the hardest days of my life (fuel)?

Being called fat. Having all of the journalism school professors at my college sign a petition to have me removed because I wasn't their first choice for editor-in-chief. My boss not believing in my vision for improving his business with a publication and with the addition of social media.

How did I overcome them (fuel)?

With the help of great people. I must associate myself with great people in order to accomplish my vision.

What are the key characteristics I used to overcome them (fuel)?

Belief in myself and my capabilities. Persistence and the willingness to do whatever it took to accomplish something great. A positive attitude.

Who will help me win this goal (people)?

My parents. Industry supporters—franchise consultants who demand more for their clients. Industry friends who are entrepreneurs, too, as they know what I am going to go through.

How can they fuel my vision (people)?

When I run into tough situations, I will be open and honest with them. I will listen very carefully to their advice. Should I struggle financially or get in a bind, I can ask them for support.

What does the end look like (belief)?

Running a successful agency, an agency that disrupts the traditional meaning of an agency.

———

Now it's your turn. Your vision is what you want to accomplish. We have talked about it, and by now, hopefully you have thought about what you want to accomplish. Is it running your first half marathon, starting a business, buying a franchise? How do you create your vision?

When I was in elementary school, I thought I was going to be a baseball player. Sure, I loved the entrepreneurial businesses that I was creating at the time, but I loved them for the money that I could make. In high school, my vision was to be a sports writer, combining my love for writing and sports. In college, my vision was to be a music/entertainment writer, which evolved into starting my own business—an online magazine. After college, that vision continued. I took a job in public relations to learn more about the intersection of business and a magazine. I presented that vision to my boss. He told me no. My vision changed to starting my own agency.

It's OK for your vision to change over time. You may start off with a vision to run a half marathon and evolve to participate in a triathlon as you learn more about your vision when in the action phase. You may decide that you want to buy a franchise but change your vision to create a franchise as you learn that you could do it differently and better.

Planning and being prepared will help you understand how to create action within your vision.

What is your next vision? Write it down in one simple definitive headline (No Limit Media Consulting, a social media/public relations boutique communications agency).

Work through the following:

What is the business I want to create or goal I want to accomplish?

Why am I creating this?

What do I expect to happen?

Rework your foundation equation: fuel + people + your belief. Build out your story:

What in my past has helped me prepare to start this (fuel)?

What have been the hardest days of my life (fuel)?

How did I overcome them (fuel)?

What are the key characteristics I used to overcome them (fuel)?

Who will help me win this goal (people)?

How can they fuel my vision (people)?

EXERCISE

Continued

What does the end look like (belief)?

After answering these questions, you then should do your category projections. This will help you define your goals— which can be used for both business and personal.

Plan

What is your plan? What are your points of differentiation? What is your pathway to profits?

People

Who will be your influencers? How will they help drive your profits? Who will be your stars? How will you keep them?

Places

Where will you market? How will you market? How will you tell your story?

Projected Win

How do you define your win? Is it money, is it losing weight? What does the victory look like? How are you going to make money or achieve personal happiness profit? What will define happiness?

Even if you are currently at the so-called top, involved in a business as the visionary or the leader, or winning but wanting to take your goal to the next level, working through the previous exercise can help frame and visualize your fuel and purpose. As you work through your plan, engage your people, understand your places, and earn your profit, you will have to repeat this process over and over again.

It will be interesting to look in the rearview mirror and see how many rewrites you made of your plan, how your life transpired, and how fuel was created. You should start to see connected dots. For me, when I look in that rearview mirror, I see a few news publications, I see communications, I see technology, and I see marketing. These are all pieces that, when added up, are still valuable to my entrepreneurial story. Each piece of the puzzle that may have not made a lot of sense at the time has now collectively turned into my agency's trade publication and content marketing platform, 1851Franchise.com.

Many entrepreneurs find that they have started, stopped, and failed many times before finding the first gem that has all four winning parts: plans, people, places, and profits. My story has been similar. I share with you these stories to help guide you to remembering yours and leveraging the steps in your journey to make your next step stronger. When deciding on your next big idea, it is important to rely on the experiences of the past, as they will guide you through your decisions, help you identify your passions, find your stream of positivity, and ultimately lead you to your personal vision, built from fuel, people, and your belief.

Reflecting on the process of creating my first few visions/businesses, I realized that they were my idea factories, my test labs. I was learning from each experience and trying to find ways to drive more net profit. At that point, clearly, I didn't understand all the ins and outs of the business, but I was able to build upon the success of the previous challenge.

When you are creating your vision, you may begin to see links to previous experiences. In the moment, those experiences/visions are real. In the past, they turn into the laboratory phase—trials and errors.

Those early moments of identifying the foundation and building upon it probably need a little naiveté. Not knowing everything or enough helps one believe that anything is possible and allows one to be more exploratory and take more risks.

When reflecting on my entrepreneurial journey, the interesting thing about each of my other visions (I will tell you more stories later) is that they taught me a little more about the fundamentals of business. Each time I created something that didn't meet my vision, I felt like a failure in the moment, when in reality, I was building my fundamentals.

FUNDAMENTALS

Fundamentals are critical to accomplishing your vision. They will help lead you to your big aha moment.

Far too often entrepreneurs unnecessarily complicate things by forgetting about the basics. They focus on the chaos instead of the fundamentals. This is natural, because many of us feed on fixing drama versus further investing into what's known and working. When we forget about the basics, it becomes challenging to build momentum and ultimately start rolling your entrepreneurial velocity. Velocity is built after doing the fundamentals really well, pulling up to momentum, and owning it.

In 2006 I hired a personal trainer. Prior to starting our workout regimen, I walked through my vision. My vision was to dunk a basketball at the end of the year, as I loved playing the sport and loved the physical activity it drove me to participate in.

To help battle my weight issues, I played two times per week with two different groups to ensure my commitment to cardio was established. This engagement with a personal trainer would hopefully lead to a magical moment—me stealing the ball, hustling down the court, taking a leap off of my dominant foot, dunking the ball, and grabbing the rim. My peers would look on in disbelief.

My fuel was still being called fat. My people was my trainer. I believed that if I stayed committed to my trainer's prescribed process, I would be able to dunk a basketball. My vision was to dunk that ball.

As the year went on, I stayed committed to each step of my trainer's process. I noticed some wins, in that I could now grab the rim versus just touch it. But still I couldn't dunk. At the end of the twelve months, I was ready. During a pick-up game, I stole the ball, hustled down the court, leaped off my dominant leg, and ricocheted the ball off the tip of the rim.

I couldn't dunk.

My vision had failed. I was deflated.

I went back to my trainer that Monday and told him the story. He said, "I didn't think you were going to be able to dunk." I said, "Why didn't you tell me?" He said he didn't want to let me down and "the only way you will be able to dunk the ball is if you were to lose another thirty pounds."

I was stronger than I had ever been. The fundamentals of my game were actually better, as I was playing better defense, passing sharper, and rebounding better.

While that moment didn't lead to me seeing my vision the way I had hoped, it did add a lot of value to my athletic and physical appearance.

I owned it. I improved my foundation for my vision, but I recognized that I would not have the skills or the foundation to achieve my belief. So, I settled on other half-full moments.

Think about baseball. Think about the greatest pitchers in the game today. Are they much bigger than you? Are they much stronger than you? Probably not. But they probably understand the fundamentals better than you or I do, whether naturally or through years of proper coaching. In sports, this understanding is the ultimate difference between good and great.

In life, even if you don't achieve your ultimate goal, there is plenty of value in the fundamentals of the process.

As I continued my path toward creating true entrepreneurial velocity, I decided to build upon the businesses that I had created and leverage the things I felt were ultimately valuable. This way, I could truly learn from my mistakes and constantly reflect on how I could leverage those learnings to make them magical.

Not every business hit the vision statement that I wrote out; however, I started to leverage the learnings. I continued to develop the fundamentals until I could apply them to a great business. There is importance in finding value even when you don't win the way you expected.

I failed at discovering the path over and over again. But, in retrospect, each failure was fuel. Would I have achieved the success I have with a carnival business or a newspaper or a music magazine? No, but those moments served as the fundamental foundation, and as I was able to leverage my personal wins and losses, the picture became clearer. My vision became clearer.

CHAPTER 5

Connecting Your Story to Your Vision

With any vision, you will need a plan, people, places, and projected profits to have a truly defined blueprint for your own success. In this chapter, I've included a few examples of how I apply the complete foundational equation to my vision. As you read through these, think about how you want to apply the process to your own vision. Your own vision will be important as we move to the next part of the equation.

KID'S NEWS: BUILDING BUSINESS FUNDAMENTALS

As a day-dreaming fourth grader, I often thought about possibility and opportunity. Possibility in what I could become and opportunity in what I could create. I was constantly thinking about ways to make money. I created many business concepts, all of which came from seeing a gap opportunity. A gap opportunity is when you take something that is already created and make it better (which you will see are most of my business concepts).

At my elementary school, Longfellow in Oak Park, Illinois, there was no school newspaper. I saw this as an opportunity to deliver the news to my school. Think of it as a *People* magazine for the fourth grade—and remember, this is in the late eighties.

Much like any blueprint, I initially worked through my vision with a fellow classmate. Zack was really good at drawing. I knew we could leverage his art skills to form our publication. But I also knew the easiest pathway to great stories was to build a team of storytellers. We knew we couldn't create a publication alone, as we didn't have the ability to produce all the content while creating the design, executing the distribution, managing the marketing, and running the company. We started recruiting others—explaining our vision for this publication we were going to call *Kid's News*.

Most of the kids in our class were in. However, there was one, Rachel, who wanted to compete. She too saw an opportunity to create her own publication. Competition can be good.

With *Kid's News*, I had some fuel, some people (seed money from my parents and friends), and great belief. I had a vision and the guts of a plan. My vision, in this case, was less about money and more about status and building relationships. I was also comfortable with being called an entrepreneur as I had learned it was not a grandma insult but rather someone believing in me. I had my *Kid's News* blueprint, too, modeling it as a mini version of the *Chicago Tribune* geared for kids.

Vision

Create the best news publication for Longfellow Elementary School in Oak Park, Illinois. This publication would mirror a newspaper, in that it would have news, lifestyle, comics, sports, and business. It would be Xeroxed at a local convenience store, and each monthly copy would sell for $.25. I would use my parents' money to pay for the publication and would use the money made to host an epic kickball pizza party at my parents' house. My vision was to become the most popular kid in school, overcoming previous bullying and ensuring that no one would think of me as the fat kid anymore but rather as cool, smart, and innovative (even though I doubt I knew that word then). They would begin referring to me as an entrepreneur.

People

I would need writers, illustrators, and those who would help me distribute the publication. With my dad being a pro at the computer, I would leverage him for print-ready design and my mom for copy editing. They would be paid nothing, as they were in the family— and, according to my fourth-grade mindset, family members should never be paid. Here, I had people who were supporters and professional resources for helping me achieve my vision.

Places

The publication would initially be distributed to the school. I would then sell it to the *Chicago Tribune* for millions (dream big).

Projected Profit

We would print two hundred copies and make $.25 per copy. This would equal $50, enough to buy the pizzas and make me rich.

Outcome

Kid's News was wildly successful by kids' standards.

The first issue was about ten pages, which cost roughly $.50 to print. We sold $50 worth of publications at $.50 each. We were rich (except for that part where we had to use my parents' money to pay for the printing).

We also won against the other publication. Rachel created competition, but she couldn't find enough people to help her. We were also first to market, and everyone wanted to be a part of my publication.

Our exit wasn't as glorious as I had hoped, as the *Chicago Tribune* would not buy the publication for millions, because they already had a professional section (that I swear launched after ours) called *Kidz News*. I did, however, throw an epic kickball and pizza party with that $50, and for a few weeks, I wasn't called fat.

What I Would Do Differently

I would have charged more for the publication. I would have printed it on one single page front and back, folding it in half to save money. I would have printed more copies and distributed them to the local library and sports facilities to help with distribution—or convinced one of the neighborhood kids who distributed the local community paper to insert it into the existing papers for added marketing. I would have limited the staff to increase the demand of those wanting to work for it. And I would have been more thankful to my investors, my parents, for backing it financially—along with pretty much every other business I ever created.

Foundationally, this attempt acted as a key ingredient of the equation. This was a part of the fuel in my foundation. Again, failure is OK, as long as you learn from it and eventually recognize it as positive. In the moment, it can be challenging to understand the value of failure, but upon later reflection, you may be able to leverage those moments for your benefit.

Now think about you. Really, stop and think. Think about a business or a goal you ultimately failed at. Reflect. Whether it's starting a business that didn't reach your initial vision or trying to dunk a basketball, walk through the previous prompts to find your silver linings. After thinking about it—write that moment down. Store it. You will want that fuel later. It will help you identify fundamentals from previous experiences that will propel your next one.

Vision

What was your vision?

What were your points of differentiation?

What was your pathway to profits?

EXERCISE

Continued

People

Who were your influencers?

How did they help drive your profits?

Who were your stars?

How did you keep them?

Places

Where did you market?

How did you market?

How did you tell your story?

Projected Profit

How did you make money or achieve personal happiness profit?

How much did you project to make?

How much did you need to make to be happy?

What Would I Do Differently?

In my next business, I tried to leverage my experiences from the previous attempt.

CARNIVAL ROUND ONE

As a fifth grader, my dreams only widened. Starting a newspaper was great, but starting a carnival would be greater.

I admired the community carnival/Village Day that would happen each year in my town. At these events, the game I admired most was bouncing a Ping-Pong ball into a fish bowl, which would often drive hundreds of kids to line up with the dream of owning their very own pet fish (of course, not realizing that the typical life expectancy of a goldfish was probably only a few short days). This game always intrigued me, as did the speed pitch game and the dunk tank, though it provided no ROI for the thrower other than the pure enjoyment of dunking a person.

I decided that I could create a carnival. This time, I would skyrocket the profitability. Much like the newspaper business, I knew I couldn't do it on my own. Thus I recruited my brother to be my business partner. Although he had just finished kindergarten, he had many friends on our and surrounding blocks, so I knew his pull would be valuable to driving us to millions.

Knowing I wouldn't be able to secure the equipment necessary to have the traditional carnival games and rides, we created our own version of a carnival.

From a timing standpoint, I decided to capture guaranteed foot traffic by planning an early summer carnival tied to my block's annual end-of-school party.

Vision

Create a single carnival game, which I decided would be bag toss (much like cornhole or bags today) for my initial test, and charge $1 per toss. If the participant sunk the bag, they would get $2 in return. I would start the game around the midpoint of the block party dinner, when kids started getting itchy to do something else and before it was dark enough to play Ghost in the Graveyard.

People

I needed only one employee, my brother. AJ would get a few dollars of profit in exchange for handling my sales and marketing. AJ would be charged with getting kids to ask their parents for $1 to spend on my game. He would also police the gaming area to help the kids form a line. Of course, AJ would rely on his patrol mobile, his Power Wheels Jeep, to protect the project.

Places

We would market all day. We would use guerilla-marketing tactics to excite the neighborhood about a bags-for-cash game later in the night. We would also position the game in the middle of the block, providing the greatest opportunity to secure as many dollars as possible—including from the parents, who would feel obligated to spend $1 and miss, since there were two little kids running the program.

Projected Profit

We would make thousands of dollars, which, in turn, I would spend on baseball cards and, in turn, sell to become a millionaire.

Outcome

We made money—in fact, we made close to $50. This was incredible, as the overhead was $5 to AJ, there was no seed money from an investor, and the game was challenging enough that kids wanted to try multiple times to win. The challenge was, it wasn't the thousands of dollars I had predicted, and I wouldn't become an instant millionaire. However, what I did learn is scalability and how I could constantly build upon the initial success I found.

What I Would Do Differently

I could add more games for the second block party and market outside of our block (believing that every kid loved a block party). I may have charged more, but I knew I was testing out my carnival game planning. As a fifth grader, I was ahead of my time in proof of concept. This was clear. This was another piece of the foundation.

As the summer progressed, I decided that although AJ was a good business partner, I needed a more seasoned partner in order to amplify the results. AJ's reach was good—he had cornered the audience on our block and would still be valuable to my master plan for carnival rounds two and three—but I decided to pull in someone else. I picked a kid from my class named Zach (not Zack, who helped me with *Kid's News*).

Zach lived a few blocks away and clearly had an in with a crowd I didn't. His crowd was made up of nerdy kids who loved *Star Wars* (before it was obviously cool) and the card game Magic. What the dorky kids had that the middle-of-the-pack kids didn't was money. They saved. They had those awesome quarter counters that stacked quarters up to $100. I wanted one of those—the problem was I took every dollar I made and invested it in day trading (baseball cards).

Zach, of course, was instantly interested in being my business partner—especially after I apologized for teasing him and offered him a 50/50 split of revenue. The difference here was that I would need $20 of seed investment money to pay for the prizes and printing of fliers. With his cash, my idea and drive, and our collective networks, we were going to create an epic carnival.

CARNIVAL ROUND TWO

Use the end-of-summer block party for the second run. Increase the reach of the carnival by adding on an investor/partner, who would invest $20 to cover the expenses of prizes and printing. Market the carnival significantly in advance (six weeks) so that kids could get the August carnival on their calendars and have something to look forward to, similar to block parties and community carnivals. Leverage the single game R&D as the foundation for going from one to five games. Add in the goldfish component, along with an accuracy pitching game, Bozo buckets, water balloon toss, and the beanbag game.

People

AJ would still get paid a few dollars for his support, along with free games. Zach would be charged with distributing fliers throughout the community, alongside me, as well as recruiting his friends to attend the carnival.

Places

We would host the carnival on my block, utilizing the potential of return visits from my neighbors so that they were willing to pay more. The demand would be higher with the expectations and reviews from the R&D process. We would also market the carnival to all area businesses, asking them to help two kids out by posting a flier (designed in-house, by me) in their windows. It helped that my next-door neighbor was the owner of a popular children's shop, The Magic Tree Bookstore.

Projected Profit

If we made $50 from one game, we should make $250 from five games—or more because of the fish component.

Outcome

The carnival was wildly successful. While we did not hit our projected profit, Zach and I each walked away with $100 after paying AJ $10. The one snag was that we didn't take into consideration that August is really hot; fish in cups in hot weather over a three-hour period may not survive the day. We did not buy a surplus of $.50 fish, which could have helped us make money when they died. It also didn't help that I was afraid to touch the dead fish, so the shriek I let out when trying to remove them was not good.

What I Would Do Differently

Kids were hungry and thirsty, so we would have added a concessions component. Also, the pitching game had to be in the backyard due to space restrictions (front yard), away from the block party, which did not create enough demand. I also realized that the reach of this carnival was still restricted to people on the block and at our elementary school. Reach needed to be expanded. However, earning $100 was nice. Zach got the better part of the deal. While he did the same amount of work as I did, it was my idea. He simply had to work hard and invest $20 to get an equal $80 in return. We remained friends, though, and I stopped teasing the dorky kids as I realized they could provide long-term value to me.

While each of the first two carnivals had its fair share of failures, they also created fuel from learned experiences. Our carnivals were not perfect; they did not achieve the ultimate success we had hoped for, but I coupled our learnings and applied them to the next go. I used our misses and our wins as fuel. I also learned from testing baseline elements in each version of the business and taking advantage of the support structures that help take a business from good to great. These included the following:

Capital

It takes money to make money. You don't need a ton to be successful, but the more seed money you have, the better you will feel about the work you are doing. The money almost acts as a validator. If you can build a strong reserve, you can use that to make your next business move—all while growing your current business.

Partner

This is a tough one. Having a partner can help to offset the work, but so can lower-cost partners who act as employees. For me, it was very costly percentagewise to have a business partner in each of my ventures. I gave away the farm without requiring much. I did get a great, hardworking employee out of it—but in exchange for a ton of equity.

Reach

Reach is vital. Without buzz, nothing gets off the ground. Some of the greatest concepts are just that until more people find out about it and talk about it. *Kid's News* was successful because of the epic party I was going to throw. People talked about it. The carnivals were strong and continued to grow as more and more people found out about them.

Marketing

Marketing was critical—and ultimately the most important piece of the puzzle. However, there is a great lesson to be learned about marketing. Without great operations, marketing will be meaningless. If we pulled in a record number of customers but didn't have enough goldfish to reward them for sinking the ball, customers would be left unhappy and would leave the carnival.

PR

This is extremely valuable and, when earned, can provide an invaluable amount of credibility. PR for the carnival came in the way of word of mouth and fliers snuck into the local newspaper. What would have happened if we had gotten a reporter to write about us?

CARNIVAL ROUND THREE

As I entered my third and final attempt at the carnival business, with a dream of becoming a millionaire, I decided to make a few more adjustments. This time I needed to expand my reach wider throughout Oak Park. I also needed to make sure I had the right business partner.

These were all thoughts that echoed through my head as I sat in my makeshift basement office in my parents' house. I needed space for R&D and to put up my drawings/plans on the wall. The office basement would also serve as my interviewing bunker, a secret hangout to determine who would be the next partner.

Of course, partnering with me came with the foundation of the past two events. AJ made money both times. Zach made even better money.

This time, we were going to use the June block party as the starting point, and we would start marketing while school was still in session.

To find the right business partner, I decided to conduct open interviews with a few different sets of people outside of my small network, trying to match reach, profitability, and personality together.

For my options, I selected Benny, a student at Longfellow who was on the edge of being in the most popular kids group; Jon, also a student at Longfellow, who was into sports and could access his network throughout Oak Park; Zach, figuring I would give him another shot to pitch me—plus, he was hungry enough given the cash I paid him the summer prior; and Mike, a friend of mine from baseball, who lived on the north side of Oak Park (aka the richer side). I scheduled an interview with each of them while making the others patiently wait in a waiting area of the basement.

One-by-one, I took notes on their qualities that matched what I was seeking. I asked them pressing questions—particularly about how much cash they could bring to the table and how much they projected they could bring in that day.

Ultimately, after weighing the decision carefully, I decided that Mike would be the right fit. He had the most access to capital, and being that he was on the north side of Oak Park, he had a greater access to new customers. I also offered the others free games and small shares if they wanted to participate in a smaller way.

I guess this was the formation of a nonlegal, nonbinding S-corp.

Vision

Start early and market as much as possible. Market to all baseball teams, especially when Mike and my team lost to them. Market to the other schools (Mike's school and mine). Push Benny, Jon, and Zach to market too, in exchange for free games. Improve the prizes and use Mike's $50 seed money as the basis for buying more marketing materials. Leverage Mike's network to post more fliers. Expand the games by adding a spray-in-the-face game. We cut a hole in a wood board and painted a person around it, so customers could pay to hose their friends.

People

Market to the existing audience. At this point, we had to rely strictly on word of mouth, as email marketing had yet to be invented. Leverage AJ to build upon his growing audience, give him a larger cut of concessions, and have him sell the lemonade. We branded it AJ's Lemonade. Have him sell popcorn, too. My mom makes the world's greatest popcorn, and people would easily pay for a bag of it.

Places

Expand the marketing of the carnival. Rebrand it Oak Park's Greatest Carnival, indicating that all of the community carnivals could not compete. Continue to host the carnival on my parents' property. Move the concessions to the backyard to create a pull to the back—even though tickets would be sold up front. Use real raffle tickets to add a more authentic feel to the event.

Projected Profits

With another game, concessions, a wider audience, and a growing customer base, we should easily exceed $500 in profit.

Outcome

We came close. We grossed $400. I ended up matching the $50, to give us greater prizes, which meant we each walked away with $150. It was a ton of work to only make $150, but for a sixth grader, it was well worth it.

What I Would Do Differently

At this point, after three attempts, I realized that the carnival business was a ton of work and didn't pave the way for me to become a millionaire. Sure, I took that money and invested it in baseball cards. But as any collector knows, baseball cards were overproduced in the nineties, meaning the value was not protected over time. The cards that I got autographed certainly retained their value. Having a business partner involved in both scenarios was the right choice, given the amount of work necessary to drive success, but the profits were not as high as I projected.

CONNECTING YOUR STORY TO YOUR VISION

As you recognize the pieces of your journey that fit into the foundation part of the equation, you, too, will bridge your past experiences to your current situation.

Follow the foundation part of the equation in your own journey. Start to piece together the previous exercises related to the fuel + people + belief = foundation formula to understand the makeup of your foundation.

In retrospect, it's interesting to think about how I felt about being an entrepreneur at that point in my life. It was my happy place and a long way from "I hate you, Grandma." It was one of my dreams. It was one of my visions. Although it required an incredible amount of vulnerability, it also provided a ton of reward. No one could tell me I wasn't good enough, because they didn't understand how I was becoming so successful. Kids, if they wanted to put me back into a tough place, would make fun of my weight, and that hurt. Also, in retrospect, I wish I'd applied the same process to my weight challenges as I did to my businesses. I was learning confidence in one part of my life but failing to apply it to the other—the different part of the vision, the personal.

Your vision can be applied to both aspects of your life—personal and professional. Professionally, I wanted to be an entrepreneur. Personally, I wanted to lose weight.

How do you develop a vision and a blueprint for a plan like that? The same way you would for a business. In vision creation and reflection, you can see how a present plan compares to the actual results. This would be the version of my plan in high school:

- **Vision:** To lose weight earlier so that the challenges would not pose a threat later.

- **People:** My parents will support my efforts. My friends will comment on how great I look when I lose weight. Both will motivate me to gain more compliments.

- **Places:** I will leverage my own determination and love for sports. I will also look into support systems like Weight Watchers.

- **Profits:** People will stop making fun of me for being overweight. I will feel heathier. I will be a better athlete.

This planning model is so simple. Had I been able to cross-apply my business ventures to my personal life, I may have been in a different situation. That said, battling those challenges helped define me as an entrepreneur and, as I mentioned, turned into very powerful fuel. The *no* stopped having the same meaning, and ultimately, rather than me only hearing two potential answers (yes or no), I was able to hear a maybe, embrace the maybe, and become the driver of my own success.

That same success in business has led to similar successes in my personal life.

In life, there is no separation—business is personal and personal is business. Some people argue the reverse, but not me, especially now that I've seen the clear path that success is success—no matter where you apply it. When life intersects with business, you can leverage personal support and experiences to elevate the foundation as a part of your equation, no matter what your vision is.

Remember to keep your vision fresh and updated. It took me three tries at the carnival business, and I still hadn't achieved the success I dreamed about. At that point, I had two options: continue to adapt the vision or try something new. As a child serial entrepreneur, I chose the latter.

For you, while you will need to dream of the end goal, you will need to embrace the little wins in your foundational stages to start taking the steps into momentum and then velocity. Start thinking in half marathons instead of full. Start thinking in tapas instead of full meals. Establishing each part of the foundation for your ultimate greatness is critical to moving from this stage and into the momentum stage.

List three situations where you may have not completely won your vision, but when you reflect, you can see positive steps taken:

1.

2.

3.

EXERCISE

My foundation stage took time. My confidence had to be built from taking all of the bad and turning it into fuel, then using that fuel to create my vision for success, and then using my people to create my place of confidence.

I have also connected successes from previous experiences. When one success happens, I hustle for the next. As you chart your own personal path, start finding the connectors. Rely on this path as the foundation for what you want to do next and what goals you want to achieve (personally and in business), and to jump-start your success velocity. Your past is a part of you and will serve as a baseline for everything that happens in your future. Embrace it.

My past is my present. Today, I own a growing marketing/communications agency and a publication, but the pathway to get there all began with the foundation. Today, my weight is the lowest it has been since the sixth grade, and that pathway is the same. For me, I can always rely on how I felt as the fat kid. It's not a bad thing; it's just a part of the foundation for who I am as a person and what I want to accomplish with my vision.

Hopefully you came to this book with an idea of what you are trying to accomplish. Hopefully you now have a clear vision of your own foundation. It's your story. It's your recipe. It's your fuel + your people + your belief in the possibility of anything + your plan. It's your story.

Now let's launch the plan and execute momentum.

PART 2

Momentum

The day I was named editor-in-chief of Drake University's student-run newspaper, the *Times-Delphic*, was quite possibly the best day of my career up to that point.

"Nick, congratulations, you have been named editor-in-chief of the *Times-Delphic*," a board member said on a call. "We look forward to witnessing your success."

Being recognized by a university board as the next editor of the student newspaper after being beaten down by bullies, baseball coaches, writing teachers, and Will Clark—this, I perceived, was velocity. Truly making it. Pop the bubbly. Time to celebrate.

Wait, pause.

The day after that call was quite possibly the worst day of my career up to that point.

"Nick, I have some bad news," the board member said on the next call.

Nearly every journalism professor requested that I be immediately removed and that the runner-up in the presentations and hiring process be put in place instead. Why? Collectively, they disagreed with the board and felt she should be named editor. She had earned it, and in their eyes I hadn't.

Additionally, they found a loophole in the rules of the job; to serve as editor-in-chief, I needed an advisor. With all of them signing the petition, I was challenged.

"We are really sorry you have to go through this," said the board member. "None of the journalism professors will be your advisor. If you can't find someone, you may be forced to resign."

I said OK while tears rolled down my face. It was as if I was being called fat all over again. But with this incident, I reacted differently. I cried, but I didn't curl into a ball and quit. I had learned the fundamentals of dealing with bullied moments. I had experienced some successes and small wins. I had grown thicker skin as a result of my previous experiences.

Rather than quit, I was prepared to do something different: I listened. I wanted to find the silver lining, my opportunity.

As I wiped away my tears, I started calling my people, those who had my back. I called my parents, who reiterated their belief in me. I called my *Rolling Stone* friend Rich Cohen, who said no one could stop me. I talked with my friend and fellow sports writer at the paper, Jason Wells, who said it was bullshit and that he would have my back as my sports editor. I even called the newly appointed dean of the journalism school, Charlie Edwards, who said that while he couldn't be my advisor for obvious political reasons, he would give me all the advice in the world. Together, we revisited the conversation.

"They said you would only have to resign if you couldn't find a faculty advisor, right?" he said. "Don't just look in the journalism school."

My confidence was building, and despite being told I wasn't good enough, I was not giving up this time. I was pushed down, but I got back up and was confident that I would win. I had my foundation—and recognized it. This was the start of momentum.

I was awarded the position. It was mine. If I were to mess up, then they could have me removed, but I was on a mission to create something amazing.

Armed with a little confidence, I had a plan to seek advisory elsewhere. I was minoring in graphic design, which was run out of the art school. I leveraged this to ask my photography professor, a part-time professor, if she would lend her name as my advisor. She agreed.

Equipped with an advisor, I went back to the board and said I was ready for action with a plan.

Momentum can be tricky. Just when you think you are there, you can be thrust back to foundational building moments where you learn more lessons and create more fuel. Understanding the shifts in the formula will be key to your eventual success. One day I was thinking the culmination of all of my hard work as a writer had paid off; the next, I was wondering how I fell so hard.

Momentum is when you start building confidence on top of your foundational wins. Bullying begins to taper off as your confidence grows. Bullies see you as less of an easy target, and if there is bullying, it doesn't affect you as much because of your newfound confidence.

Momentum is built from confidence + one inch of difference + action. Little wins, building moments, self-definition, and action. But momentum will have some turbulence.

Foundation feeds momentum. The lessons learned from foundation can be applied to this part of the equation, too.

Vision

The *Times-Delphic*, up to that point, had not been a profit generator for the university. My plan was threefold: Make the publication profitable, increase the print runs (it published twice a week, and I wanted to deliver more to increase advertising potential), and create a signature special issue around the Drake Relays (a big event for the school).

People

My people were going to be tougher to find. Without any backing from the journalism professors, I was going to have to dig deeper and be creative to create my support structure. I would also build the best staff possible by relying on my personal network and driven, gritty fellow students to form the team.

Places

While the newspaper had traditionally lived on campus only, we would take the publication into Des Moines so that the community could rally around our news.

Projected Profit

Any profit would be a win. By this point I'd had plenty of unprofitable business ideas, but this one had built-in credibility that I could leverage.

I realized that in my journalism career, I was moving out of the foundational stages because I was able to leverage fuel, people, and my belief. Each made sense to the next stage, as I was finding my confidence, one inch of difference, and action to start exploring this newfound stage of momentum.

Momentum is a magical feeling. With momentum, after a setback, you quickly wipe away your tears and start in on the real work. Your hard work pays off, little by little, and you start truly witnessing the success of your vision. Roadblocks will continue to stand in the way, but rather than falling down, you will continue to charge forward.

Momentum, for you, will feel great, and chances are, you have experienced it in your life already. It could have been with anything—passing a test, making a sports team, writing a chapter in your book, or introducing yourself to someone you would like to meet.

Reflect on your own momentum. Think about the following:

What moment did you start recognizing some level of confidence?

What was your ultimate plan?

What was different?

What stood out?

What was winning?

EXERCISE

Continued

How did you decide to leverage it?

What were a few of those wins?

Momentum, in any of your wins, will be critical in helping you reach the break-through-brick-wall stage, otherwise known as velocity.

CHAPTER 6

Confidence

In the foundation stage, you reflected on your fuel, identified your people, and found some of your belief by becoming laser-focused on changing your perceptions. Now, in momentum, you start to take the foundational parts of the equation and maximize them.

A stronger sense of confidence develops when you execute on your beliefs and wins. In many cases, a stronger sense of confidence also involves using your creativity to build on your beliefs and wins.

When you reflect on your past to identify the working parts of the foundational equation, understand that you are not done. New foundational elements will be added whenever you try to build a new equation. When I decided my vision for *Kid's News* and saw some success, it didn't mean I was leaving the foundational side. Most of us, as humans, are constantly searching for forms of self-improvement. The foundational stage is always working in the background.

Because of your experiences up to this point, you are able to create a stronger sense of confidence. It is maximized. The added confidence is the start to the momentum stage and will be an essential ingredient to building your vision. Without it, you will never start to mature in this stage.

DON'T BE COCKY

Don't confuse confidence with cockiness, which is a false sense of confidence. Cockiness won't work in this stage. It is thinking you know everything when you don't. It is treating people as if they are less than you when you have no reason to. Being cocky can backfire and set you back to the foundational stage if you are not careful.

An important step of building confidence is knowing where the line between confidence and cockiness stands. Oftentimes, you can rely on your people to help keep you grounded. Ask your people to serve as your checks and balances.

LEVERAGE YOUR CONFIDENCE

For me, not every situation comes with confidence. Sometimes, in order to win, I have to leverage the confidence that I have with the belief that I can achieve success in a particular moment. Confidence is something you will always try to build upon. Confidence is the critical characteristic to those who achieve success.

When reflecting on moments in your past, quite often you will see confidence even though you might not have felt confident at the time. It could be how you felt after you got a hit in baseball, how you felt when you saw your byline in print, how you felt when a girl didn't completely ignore you.

Each experience in life, successful or not, is one more step toward achieving whatever you are setting out to accomplish. Many people leverage fuel moments to become a better version of themselves. In business, those at the top have relied on their past fuel experiences to help identify their true points of differentiation and opportunities—and to help coach them through difficult decisions.

BE CREATIVE

When it comes to establishing a stronger sense of confidence and turning nos into maybes, the easiest way to guide you toward finding your own internal story is to use the plan similar to the one I used to secure a girlfriend as a first grader.

We are conditioned to believe that when it comes to winning with girls, fat kids always finish last. And nice is always trumped by fat. With the little confidence I had, I wanted to prove that condition wrong. As a fat kid, I needed something more than charm to find a girlfriend.

Starting in first grade, my neighbor Danny and I were best friends. We were a dynamic duo. By dynamic, I mean that I would ride the coattails of Danny's charm, good looks, and kid-muscular physique to hopefully find a girlfriend. This plan would work as long as Danny would remain my wingman.

Danny certainly had the upper hand with girls. He probably already had protruding muscles in first grade, which meant that my best friend could beat your best friend's ass (another sign of a good support person). I, on the other hand, had to use creativity to convince girls to be my girlfriends.

My heart fell in love with Ruth, a freckle-faced first grader who looked nearly identical to my celebrity crush, Punky Brewster. And Ruth was a first grader whom Danny hadn't shown interest in. He preferred blond over dark hair, thus leaving me wide open with no competition for Ruth.

With the courage gained from Danny's pep talks on our four-block walk to school, I decided to ask her out.

Asking someone out in the first grade meant nothing more than proclaiming the girl you hung out with at recess was your girlfriend—all while being conflicted over whether to play basketball, football, or tag with the boys or hang out and play in the sandbox with the girls.

A rush of happiness overcame me.

"Ruth, would you be my girlfriend?" I asked.

"If you buy me a Cabbage Patch Kid, I will be your girlfriend," she said.

Buy her a Cabbage Patch Kid? How was I going to do that? I didn't have a car. I didn't have an older brother or sister who owned one. I never even liked those stupid dolls.

Making Ruth my girlfriend was going to be a challenge.

"I will make this happen," I replied.

That weekend, I went on a secret mission to obtain a Cabbage Patch Kid.

I knew the key to toys was chores. Hard work equals great return, *most of the time.* I very calmly asked my mom if there was anything I could do to earn a trip to Toys"R"Us. She listed out the options, including feed the dog, make my bed, clean up my room, and play with my brother. I was willing to do all of these things for love.

Saturday morning came, and I went to work. My vision, if executed, meant that my hard work would earn me a trip to Toys"R"Us. I would have to showcase some shifted energy away from my typical purchase, then I would give Ruth the earned toy, and then I would fall in love, get married, and live happily ever after. Ah, the vision of a little kid.

As we made our way to the store, I began to mastermind my magical toy switch. I am sure at this point my mom was thinking I would ask her to buy me Matchbox Cars, baseball cards, or some kind of trinket for my bike.

As we walked down the doll aisle, I stopped and pointed to one. "Mom, this is what I want," I said in a very confident tone.

I'm sure it was an extremely puzzling moment for her—and even worse for my dad when we returned with the doll. Luckily, the doll would quickly disappear.

I packed that pretty doll in my bag on Monday morning, and off to school we went. I explained to Danny the purpose of the doll and forever strengthened our childhood friendship. He knew I was sneaky—committed to finding my confidence. He knew I was a man. He knew I had found a way around my fatness and into the heart of the Punky Brewster look-alike.

I recognized his confidence in me. It was time for a taste of momentum. As we approached the playground, I slowly unzipped my backpack, knowing that I would see Ruth within a few minutes. I reached in my bag, pulled out the doll, and handed it to her.

Her puzzled face quickly turned into a smile. She was now my girlfriend.

Sure, you may laugh, but that was "winning" for the fat kid. The fat kid in me wanted to show the world that I, too, could "get" a girlfriend. The fat kid in me wanted to prove that there were more parts of attraction than just looks. The fat kid, in the moment, didn't understand that confidence builds confidence, but he did understand the value in finding strength in strengths—including humor, confidence, and the true belief that anything is possible. The fat kid, while not recognized at the time, was ready to use the fuel and make something out of it.

My relationship with Ruth wasn't a long one, and for first graders, it was quite complicated. She introduced me to her friend Kristen and said it was OK if Kristen was my girlfriend too. Kristen told me she didn't want a doll; she wanted a stuffed animal. I had plenty of those and plenty to steal from my brother. I turned into the kid who could make the dreams of girls happen (I had a lot of them in the first grade, thanks to my trade-for-date vision), and in exchange, I was able to hide my fatness for one more year.

In your own life, you probably have similar stories, ones that involve your use of creativity for wins.

Sometimes, a little creativity can help you get around the challenges that you face and build some confidence.

As you continue to think about your next vision—whether in life or in business—think back to your Ruth moments as a kid. These are the moments where you identified an opportunity, refused to be deterred, took encouragement from your people, used what you learned from your past experiences, and showcased creativity.

Smile about those moments. Find some more confidence in them. Find some happiness in the fact that you had a win. Think about how you felt, and try to get back to that point, to that feeling. With a stronger sense of confidence, you will be one inch closer to jumping off your hypothetical ledge of working toward your next great vision.

CHAPTER 7

One Inch of Difference

By this point, you should have recognized the foundation you have built and are beginning to recognize the momentum you are starting to gain with your stronger sense of confidence. You have the start of a vision and are now trying to piece together your story and your moments that will lead you to accomplish something great.

After confidence comes the points of differentiation, which I call your one inch of difference. You will need this in order to stand out with whatever you are trying to accomplish.

One inch, just one inch—think about the value of just being slightly better than the next person or competition. It could be the difference of the basketball going into the hoop, a golf ball in the hole, the bat hitting the ball, the football being caught for a touchdown. It could be the difference between writing a book, starting a business, or avoiding the plate of cookies on the counter. It could be the difference between being in the right place at the right time and winning the slot machine, catching a foul ball, getting a first-class upgrade.

You only need one inch of difference. Just one.

In life, one inch of difference can mean winning rather than losing. It can be that X factor that helps you build your confidence, plan, and execution. It can be the reason why people believe in you or your brand.

That one inch will be important to winning the next step of momentum. That one inch can be found in one's self, in one's idea, or in one's business. When building your plan, identifying the key one inch of difference is critical. With it, you are in a great position to establish your foundation, ignite your momentum, and spark your velocity.

With Ruth, I found ways around my limitations with humor and creativity. I was able to build on my confidence and add in my one inch of difference—my ability to get a Cabbage Patch Doll for her.

Being successful in life is all about finding your one inch of difference. That one simple, small inch is what will help define your path to standing out. Whether you dream of becoming a millionaire or you simply dream of a stress-free life full of simple happiness, your one inch is how you will find it. No one but you—not your husband, wife, father, mother, sister, brother, son, daughter—can dictate your one inch. It is yours, and yours only, to decide how much of a difference your next step can potentially mean for your life.

Think about a hitter. Someone who gets three hits out of every twelve at bats will make a few million dollars per year. Someone who gets four hits out of every twelve at bats (a .333 average) will make tens of millions of dollars per year. Just one more hit per twelve at bats.

An example of this can be seen in the difference between two players who played a significant time in Major League Baseball, one of whom was a Hall of Famer and one who was not.

Hall of Famer Ty Cobb, whose career ended in 1928, has the highest career average hits at .366. He collected 4,189 hits in his twenty-four-year career.

There are approximately six months (twenty-four weeks) to a baseball season. Cobb played twenty-four seasons; this means he played 576 weeks. During that time, he

- had 7.27 hits per week

- played 3,034 games

- had 1.38 hits per game

- had 11,434 at bats

- had a batting average of .366

Julio Franco collected 2,586 hits over his career that ended in 2007. Franco played twenty-four seasons, which means he played 552 weeks. During that time, he

- had 4.68 hits per week

- played 2,527 games

- had 1.02 hits per game
- had 9,731 at bats
- had a batting average of .298

The difference between Franco and Cobb was less than three total hits over a week and 62.16 total hits a season. Just three hits a week is the difference between a Hall of Fame player and someone who was good and sustainable but certainly not legendary.

In today's game, the difference between staying in the game and getting paid is one hit per week. The difference between a .250 and .300 is twenty-five hits over 500 at bats. That's all.

When it comes to life, business, and sports, one simple inch can make the greatest difference in the outcome of your plan. As you read this, think about your one inch. Think about how the challenges you have faced in life have prepared you for this moment. That, my friends, is a big part of your momentum. Blend in your earned and experienced fundamentals and you are ready to start your next journey.

When it comes to creating your momentum for your business, identify that inch you will need. When it comes to unifying your personal plan, identify that inch, too.

HOW DO YOU FIND YOUR ONE INCH?

When I am speaking at conferences, I like to start with an exercise that helps lead people to thinking about their one inch. While the exercise is challenging to perform in a book, I will explain the details and then share with you some questions you should ask yourself when adding the one inch of difference to your approach.

I instruct the audience to write down as many numbers as they can. I also tell them that the most important thing to do is write responses to my three commands.

The speed of the numbers is to simulate their busy lives—work, children, chores, church, sports, and so on. In between the sets of numbers, I ask the audience to write down a color, a piece of furniture, and then a genius.

I tell the audience to stand and then sit if they put down a basic color. Naturally, the majority of the colors are red, white, blue, green, orange, purple, pink. Those few people who have written colors like turquoise or magenta remain standing.

Everyone stands again. The furniture responses are similar to the colors. Those who chose chair, bed, desk, table, couch, or sofa sit down. Armoire is the typical one that a few who will remain standing will say.

Finally, the genius. I tell them to sit down if they said Albert Einstein, Thomas Edison, or Steve Jobs. A few will remain standing. With the audience's eyes stuck on these select few, I instruct those who wrote themselves to sit down. Most, in that case, do.

What's the purpose? It's very difficult to find your standout moments or your one inch of difference when your life is so busy, stressful, and heavy. Thus, it is important to get away from life, even for a moment, to think about how you can stand out in your vision. It's not easy.

For you, you have an idea of what you want to accomplish. What I would like you to do is put down the book for five minutes and think about what will make you different.

FIVE-MINUTE THINK PAUSE

In the recent business world, we have seen self-serve frozen yogurt explode and then disappear because there were zero points of difference among the various brands of yogurt and the toppings and the overall experience. The same can be said about fast-casual pizza.

I have constantly searched for that one inch of difference in my personal and professional lives.

After earning a little confidence from my Will Clark moment, I needed my one inch of difference to make my *Rolling Stone* moment turn into momentum. My one inch of difference came when I spoke up and took the internship into my own hands. I came prepared. I had a stronger sense of confidence. I wanted to show arguably some of the world's top editors that I was all in when it came to story building and storytelling.

Logically, after the summer of Will Clark, I returned to Drake University to march through my sophomore year—the whole time dreaming about what my upcoming internship opportunity would include. In order to have options to weigh, I applied for two other internships—getting both of them—the *Kansas City Star* on the sports desk and *Playboy* on the editorial team.

But, true to his word, Cohen granted me a once-in-a-lifetime opportunity to attempt making *Almost Famous* real with an internship at *Rolling Stone* magazine in New York City.

The *Rolling Stone* internship was three days a week, so Cohen went even further, helping me secure another internship at *Details* magazine—which ended up being my *Almost Famous* connection more so than *Rolling Stone*—on the other two days.

Although prestigious in name, Rolling Stone was not as prestigious in kindness to my career. Rolling Stone ended up being my bully; Details ended up being my friend. Rolling Stone and Details, collectively, were the source of a ton of momentum for me during that summer of 2001.

At Rolling Stone, the editors were bullies. Perhaps they were continuing a hazing cycle; they had been hazed, thus they would haze the intern. If that was the case, my hazing seemed worse than that of the other interns. Perhaps they considered me the privileged intern, having snuck in through the Rich Cohen backdoor. Even so, the abuse sucked—from being the only intern who had to get the editors breakfast every day and learning that the editors invited all of the other interns to see Dave Matthews Band backstage (my favorite band at the time) to being told at the end of the summer that they would not provide me with a letter of recommendation because I spent too much energy on Details.

I *had* spent more energy at Details because the work and the editors there gave me my momentum. Rolling Stone gave me more bullying fuel for my foundation.

In week two at Details, I was invited into an editorial planning meeting. My direct supervisor strictly reminded me to sit quietly in the corner and not say anything. But there was no way I was going to waste the opportunity. Sometimes you have to weigh the risks and rewards of opportunities. Sometimes you have to notice your one inch of difference, use it with your confidence, and create an action.

As the meeting neared the end that afternoon, the editor-in-chief, Dan Peres, asked if anyone had anything else.

My hand went up.

"Who the fuck are you?" He didn't say it as harshly as Will Clark had, but he certainly was not amused.

"I am Nick, the new intern," I said as my supervisor looked at me in shock.

"OK, Nick the intern, what do you have to add?" Peres asked.

I had prepared for this moment. My vision at these internships was to get a chance to tell a story—to write something people would care about. My one inch of difference came from my willingness to speak up and my preparedness in story-idea brainstorming prior to the meeting.

"I have this idea of writing a story that connects all of the members of the Beach Boys together," I said. "Did you know John Stamos was a Beach Boy? Did you know there are several bands currently touring as former members of the Beach Boys? Did you know that Weezer is a huge fan of the Beach Boys? There are a million connections to arguably one of the greatest American bands of the sixties, and I would like to connect those dots in a family tree sort of way."

He thought it over and then said, "I like it. See what you can piece together."

A smile stretched across my face from ear to ear. Someone who'd been told he wrote at a fifth-grade level was going to have a shot to write for a national magazine. Eat it, bullies of the past.

As we exited, my supervisor said that what I did took balls. In retrospect, I would have probably handled the situation with a little more finesse and maturity. I'm sure you too when reflecting on past moments consider how you would act differently now. I wish I had known the difference between cockiness and confidence at the time.

Regardless, looking back, I realize that I finally took some of my fuel, grit, attitude, and hustle and applied it. And in doing so, I experienced a small win.

Over the next few weeks, I started interviewing various connections of the band—Carnie Wilson, Wendy Wilson, Al Jardine, sons, daughters, friends, musicians—each one connecting me to someone else who had a relationship with the Beach Boys.

Eventually, I got connected to a guy named Jeff Foskett, who was the band leader for Brian Wilson—arguably the best songwriter ever. Jeff and I hit it off during our phone interview, and he said, "You know, Brian isn't doing interviews right now, but I bet I could get you in with him. Would you like to fly to our next show for a sit down?"

Uh, hell yes.

I went to my editor on the project, Brian Farnham, who approved the travel—which conveniently happened to be to Milwaukee and Chicago over the Fourth of July weekend. It would be a chance to see my family.

After my brother AJ and I and the photographer for Details arrived in Milwaukee and secured our backstage passes, I called Jeff, who met me with a warm smile and a hug. I had the feeling it was going to be a good journey.

Jeff walked us backstage to meet Brian. We waited while he spoke to Brian, who was warming up on the piano to open for Paul Simon that night.

"Brian isn't in the mood to do the interview right now," Jeff said. "Let's try after the show."

The photographer at this point was clearly getting frustrated. He was probably a big-time photographer, but I don't remember for sure.

Milwaukee was a bust, and in Chicago, the same events happened. After Brian's set, Jeff greeted me and my brother with another warm smile and said, "Brian is a no-go today. Can you come to St. Louis with us and we can do it there?"

I called my editor, who approved the travel but was clearly disappointed about the canceled photo shoot.

"Jeff promises we can get it all squared away in St. Louis," I said, even though an interview with Brian was nearly impossible at that point according to every other music journalist who had tried to get in front of the music icon.

In St. Louis, I invited Michael Cheney, my professor from Drake, who had left his Drake position prior to the petition signing, because he taught one of my favorite classes—The Beatles: How the Media Covered the British Invasion.

This time, I scored. With my professor sitting next to me— which he later called one of the proudest and coolest moments of his career—I interviewed Brian for the first time.

He was quiet, reserved, and spoke few words. Clearly, he was uncomfortable, and despite my youth and innocence, I hadn't earned his trust. The interview was OK but certainly didn't dive into the deep questions I had planned, as he stopped the interview about ten minutes in.

Jeff promised more time along the tour. For the next two weeks I followed, trying to gain trust and access to Wilson and his crew. His wife, Melinda, took a liking to me, even sitting with me at Craft Services for dinner multiple times.

I would not give up.

The tour got back to New York, and I was able to go on Conan O'Brien and David Letterman with Wilson and his crew (by "go on," I mean sit quietly backstage as they filmed). As a bonus, I got to spend time in O'Brien's personal office, interviewing him about Wilson, which was quite amazing.

Over the few weeks with the Wilson camp, I secured three interviews with the rock legend, which was enough to piece together a story. I made friends in Jeff Foskett, Carnie Wilson (Brian's daughter and part of Wilson Phillips), Jamie Hadaad (Paul Simon's drummer), and others who helped me navigate the summer of *Almost Famous*. Each ended up helping me leverage my one inch of difference to break into this exclusive camp.

At the end of the summer, I returned to Drake University, where I would pen my piece. I thought it turned out to be an amazing article, but September 11 happened, which prevented my Brian Wilson story from being told in a national publication because other tragic news, understandably, was more important.

Though my vision of writing a signature story for *Details* didn't come to fruition, I still learned a ton from my experiences that summer, and I realized many parts of the equation that I didn't understand before then.

I applied my fuel (still being told I wasn't a good enough writer), my people (my editors, Jeff Foskett, my professor, and

Brian Wilson), and my belief (an editor said yes). I started to find a stronger sense of confidence and battle back my cockiness. And I found my one inch of difference in my willingness to speak up and have confidence when going out on the road with one of the greatest songwriters of all time.

What about you? Think back to a moment where your vision may have not come together the way you expected, but you learned a ton. Write it down.

What did you learn from that experience?

What was your fuel?

Who were your people?

How did you establish your belief?

How did you showcase a stronger sense of confidence?

What was your one inch of differentiation?

In addition to my learnings from the Details and Rolling Stone experiences, I adjusted my vision. Rather than rely on others to decide what I could and could not cover, I decided that I would start my own magazine. My next vision was *Lumino Magazine*, an online magazine.

That summer, I learned lessons and gained momentum. Armed with a new one inch of difference from the Details idea, fuel from another no, and belief and confidence in myself through the Brian Wilson experience, I started business planning my first online magazine.

Think about your life. What was your Rolling Stone/Details moment? What was that moment where you figured out a way to stand out—not necessarily against someone else but maybe against your previous life experiences? Start thinking about your stronger sense of confidence and your one inch of difference.

CHAPTER 8

Action

Momentum is a tricky part of the velocity equation (foundation + momentum = velocity). Sometimes it's difficult to understand if you are experiencing foundation or momentum moments. However, once all parts of the equation come together, you will notice the difference—especially during the initial parts of action.

Action is when you apply your confidence and one inch of difference to create a win that feels significant. It's when you start recognizing victories within your vision.

Write down the following as it relates to a single accomplishment (losing weight, running a race, making a team, winning an award, starting a business):

What was your accomplishment?

List three examples of confidence you had that helped you accomplish it:

1.

2.

3.

What were three small wins that happened on the way to your accomplishment?

1.

2.

3.

While the previous is a reflection, it will be valuable for you to rely on it to solidify your vision for your next big win.

For me, confidence was built from the Will Clark experience, and one inch of difference from my Brian Wilson experience. It was time to take action in my ultimate goal of being an entrepreneur. I decided to create *Lumino Magazine*.

Lumino Magazine, an online music magazine I created in 2001 and launched in 2003, was my turn, in business, to try finding success. It was a culmination of fuel, belief, vision, confidence, and points of differentiation: my skillsets, my business acumen, my obsession with writing and entertainment, and my drive to become popular. In fact, it was my blue ocean, an infinite place of possibilities. At the time of its creation, I was only twenty-one years old, and I had a newly created, brick wall–destroying determination. I was determined to create an online-only publication that blended music, entertainment, politics, and sports. Imagine that *Rolling Stone* magazine and *Details* magazine fell in love and made a baby— that was the vision of *Lumino Magazine.*

The magazine got off the ground by bootstrapping. A fraternity brother created the backend and frontend design of the site. The content was created by various writers and included a feature about Mark Prior and his journey to reshape the Chicago Cubs, which mirrored the tone of Rich Cohen's *Harper's* article. We also secured interviews with Nicholas Sparks, a band called Trick Turner, and a musician who went by V-ICE (a temporary artist disguise for rapper Vanilla Ice). That issue was a milestone and the work of a very busy summer of 2002.

My dream was to create a publication that challenged the alternative publications in markets like Des Moines, Chicago, and Milwaukee. However, as I entered the role of editor-in-chief of Drake's student newspaper, they asked me to put the magazine to the side for the year. I obliged.

As I graduated college, I recruited a new developer, Jon Singer, a guy I worked with at the *Northwest Herald.* He was tech savvy and would help bring us into 2003.

We shaped the magazine to be a monthly digital (this was a time when a sense of urgency in content hadn't taken complete shape). Each month, we would put out a new focused issue. To create the content, we recruited hundreds of writers who wrote for free—in turn gaining great access to concerts, celebrities, restaurants, and clubs. Our nightlife coverage focused on Chicago, Milwaukee, Des Moines, and Indianapolis.

Our relaunch issue was quite special. We secured a one-on-one interview with Howard Dean for the cover (before his obnoxious yell) and John Kerry for the inside, along with many other politicians, celebrities, and athletes. To relaunch the first issue, the Dean campaign agreed to have him meet at a small coffee shop in Des Moines to talk about young people in business. Days before the event, the Dean campaign called and said he had another commitment and was bowing out. This was not good, especially since CNN had agreed to cover our launch, and I had disclosed to my bosses at the *Northwest Herald* that I had started a digital publication for fear they would see me being interviewed on CNN. I asked if they had any alternatives. They said they had one, but they weren't sure if I would be interested.

"We could fly in Joan Jett in his place to play an acoustic set," they said, noting she was supporting his presidential bid.

"Um, I guess that will do," I replied while thinking, *Oh hell yes! The answer is yes, yes, yes.*

To relaunch the magazine, we created T-shirts that said "Vote Lumino" and hosted Jett at the small coffee shop (Java Joes in downtown Des Moines) to a packed house. It was monumental. It was a sign that momentum was building. It was a sign that anything was possible and an opportunity to be in control of something special that gave many people (our team) opportunities to have what before had seemed like impossible experiences (backstage opportunities).

The magazine continued to gain steam through the years. We did an *Office Space* reunion issue where we interviewed virtually everyone from the cast. The night before the issue was going to launch, while Jon and I frantically edited the content, Ron Livingston made a last-minute call to me asking if he could be in the issue. Jennifer Aniston and Mike Judge were the only two no-shows.

We followed that with a *Revenge of the Nerds* reunion issue; a gay issue, addressing celebrities; a *Queer as Folk* issue; a sports issue; and a TV issue.

With readership climbing, we even made a shift to posting content daily, Monday through Friday. We added a forum for discussions. We added commenting to make stories more social and collaborative with our readers. We added blogging. We continued to find writers to write for free. We produced two winter concert series called "Jingle Your Bells," where Dada (of "Dizz Knee Land" fame) performed.

We were focused on social media and social content before social media and content marketing were a thing.

The beauty of *Lumino Magazine* was that it continued for more than ten years. The challenge was that we couldn't figure out a way to make money. Not at the concerts. Not on merchandise. Not on content.

Each turn at *Lumino Magazine* was a lesson to be learned, an opportunity for our team to sponge ideas, and a chance for me to leverage my passion for business and entertainment and, of course, my belief that anything was possible.

Nos and fails can still happen when you are in momentum. During your reflections, you have probably identified moments where, while your vision may have not been completely established, you found wins along the way. In momentum, you start to recognize the value of the experiences in real time. When those moments were happening, you knew you were doing something that would add value in the end.

When you are in the momentum stage, you react to nos and failure with a stronger sense of confidence.

When you reflect on your past, think about what moments were possible for you. Take a minute to reflect on and enjoy the wins of your past. If you are an entrepreneur working your way through the momentum stage or someone still trying to find their way in their career, their life, their marriage, or their business, reflecting on the stories of the past is an essential piece to finding your entrepreneurial or personal velocity. The past will fuel your future.

Not all was lost with *Lumino Magazine* (as you will read later). It was another stepping stone to launching my eventual business—and a stepping stone personally to building confidence and believing that anything was possible.

USING AN INCOMPLETE VISION TO SUPPORT YOUR NEXT ONE

When you are creating your vision, you should benchmark around the four key principles of great businesses: have a sound plan to get to the next level, have people to support you personally and professionally, have the places for your idea to live and succeed, and have the possibility that your business can be profitable.

For me, it took many swings and misses in order to identify the right formula to ensure that I had each of the four principles. Each time I adjust my business model or plan for the next year, three years, or ten years, I think whether the change will provide enough boom in each of the categories, and if it won't, how I can either adjust it or ditch it.

Lumino Magazine was built from confidence plus a one inch of differentiation in the marketplace (taking a magazine traditionally meant for print and delivering it in an online atmosphere, where we could cover music/entertainment/political news in a faster way and in a voice that was created by twenty-somethings). It was momentum for my building journalism and business careers.

In previous planning exercises, you began to apply a plan, people, places, projected profits, and outcome. Now, as you are in the momentum stage, you will start to see the format change and the tone morph.

Plan

Create an online, monthly publication that would eventually publish daily content. Keep a simple structure for delivering information, and give readers what they want. Connect the content to real-life scenarios, including concert series. Grow readership steadily and then create a print publication.

People

Leverage contacts built from my daily newspaper job to capture interviews with big-name celebrities. Leverage younger people looking for a chance to write, paying $0 for all content.

Places

Keep the focus simple—Chicago, Milwaukee, Indianapolis, and Des Moines, a major city and three smaller cities—so that we can track readership and gradually become more competitive in those markets.

Projected Profits

Initially, $0, but start selling advertising and bring in $10,000 per month before establishing localized print publications in each market.

Outcome

Lumino Magazine still exists (maybe, depending on when you are reading this). It is not very good in look, feel, or content, as writers and contributors got older, the burnout rate increased, and they had to pay for rent, cars, and life. In retrospect, I would have ramped up faster and owned social networking. We had video. We had content. We had people. We just did not have the fire, momentum, or velocity to be wildly successful and profitable.

And now the newly introduced momentum part of the equation:

Capital

I funded the magazine with my pocket, and trust me, that pocket wasn't deep. I used the money I made from freelance writing along with my small $29,500 salary at the *Northwest Herald* to fund the publication.

Partner

I knew nothing about Web design, so I recruited Jon to be my partner. We eventually diluted our shares to provide a tiny bit of ownership to key players, like Barry Brecheisen—our managing editor and a well-known photographer in Chicago—and our nightlife and video editor.

Reach

We got into Google News very early on, which took our monthly readership from five thousand per month to fifty thousand per month.

Marketing

We leveraged the celebrities we interviewed to tell their networks, and we gave concert tickets as a form of payment to our team. We used social media, too, including using MySpace to secure interviews with bands.

PR

We actually got a lot of buzz, including an interview with Chicago Public Radio about our *Revenge of the Nerds* issue.

Technology

We were actually way ahead of the game. We had a video news series that we called *City Vision*. We had social networking on our site (in 2004). We had a vision for the future of content—in which we would start a concert review and the fans would continue it. Our digital platform was not the best, as everything about Lumino was bootstrapped, but for a bootstrapped website, it was pretty good.

One Inch of Difference

We were localized with our content and national with our theme. There were newspapers and magazines at the local level at that time, but very few provided content the way we did. We were also produced by young people looking to make a name for themselves. We were the millennial publication before that was even a thing. We provided an outlet for writers to get eyes on their work, which ultimately helped many of them secure pretty awesome jobs.

This additional planning takes your vision and starts to apply your pathway to your ultimate win. It creates executable steps to achieve your initial parts of action.

EXERCISE

Think about a moment in your life when you were able to build on your confidence when beginning a project by bringing your point of differentiation, your one-inch difference. What was that event or success?

CHAPTER 9

Execute Your Vision

A t this point, you should understand that in order for you to enter velocity, you must build your momentum on top of your foundation. Momentum is built from your foundation and the working combination will give you a shot at velocity.

The opportunity to create velocity will not start until you start. To become great, you have to start somewhere. You have to get off the couch. You have to believe that you have the bones to win. You have to have the ability to act on your dreams.

It's not simply about wanting to lose weight; it's about doing something about it. It's not simply about wanting to create a magazine; it's about taking the steps to create it.

By this point, you should have an idea of what you want to accomplish—your vision—as well as your own life stories that will create the narrative for your formula. Each ingredient and stage takes time. And each ingredient and stage, in retrospect, will play an important part of your end win.

For me, the culmination of all of my experiences led me to mine: to create the greatest midsize communications agency that ever existed.

EXERCISE

Write down your defining vision (a defining statement/headline):

While I didn't recognize it in the moment, each stage had been building before I took a shot at creating something special. My nos started early and occurred often but eventually made complete sense to me. Those nos were fundamental in my ability to quit a job, break up with a girlfriend, and move across the country to pursue a new type of happiness: my goal of creating a successful business.

Operate your vision as though it's your last chance. Operate it as if someone else is willing to fight you to death to take everything you have built away from you. Operate it with the bullied fuel of your past.

This mentality became very clear to me while I worked at Farkus Comm, which turned out to be true momentum for my velocity in starting my own public relations business.

The biggest nos of my short career came in a streak of three. My three strikes came while at my PR job. And, frankly, they didn't have to come then. I had a job I loved, a leader I admired, and a business I was very interested in being a part of for the long term. But I still had my entrepreneurial side.

After realizing *Lumino Magazine* wasn't going to work because there really wasn't much money in the music business, my entrepreneurial spirit turned to the company I was at. The public relations agency I was at was created by entrepreneurs who happened to be partners (a husband and wife team). With partners and entrepreneurs at the top, my expectation was that they would be open to having another partner in the business if that partner could show them a pathway to more revenue. They didn't see it that way, though, and that was a challenge.

My grandma was right. I was truly and proudly an entrepreneur. Farkus didn't have a shot to fight against my momentum. I was completely motivated not only to succeed but also to outperform everyone else, and I was fueled by years of nos. My mantra was respect everyone, fear no one.

I had decided to leave the newspaper business after a few short years. As *Lumino Magazine* continued to gain steam, I figured that by taking either a job in advertising, PR, marketing, or sales, I would be able to gain some very valuable business skills to propel the magazine to a new level.

With stints at the *Chicago Tribune*, *Rolling Stone*, *Details*, *The Des Moines Register*, *Northwest Herald*, and *Lumino Magazine*, my resume was pretty solid. I clearly had built a strong path in journalism, but PR would be something new to me.

For the interview, I decided to maintain my pseudo–*Rolling Stone* rock star swagger by rolling up in my fire-engine-red Ford Mustang, leather jacket and hoop earrings intact. This certainly was not kosher for a PR firm specializing in franchising, but I didn't care. As a twenty-four-year-old, if they didn't like me for who I was, then I wasn't going to be the right fit. Was this confidence? Nope. I was still cocky at that point.

Momentum is much like new money. It can change people. At the *Northwest Herald*, I went from being told I wasn't good enough to write to being one of their top columnists. Before that, you know the story—no professor support, not a good enough writer, and called the fat kid. I had created a magazine that was gaining readers and renown. I was no longer having issues with girls. And in my short stint at the *Northwest Herald*, I took a giant step toward a healthier lifestyle in that I joined Weight Watchers and took my weight from 260 to 230. I was becoming more and more fearless and more and more confident.

The cockiness was still real. I recognized that. I still needed to soften my approach.

If I could coach my younger self into acting with a little more grace, I certainly would, but as life has continued, I have realized that the more lessons you can learn through life experiences, the better chance they will have of sticking. Our parents, teachers, friends, and mentors all try to guide us toward avoiding the same mistakes they made, but I feel that mistakes are a critical component to the momentum stage. You need them. You need to be able to rely on those challenges to help you differentiate between fuel and failure.

At this point in my life, people were becoming more supportive of me. I felt less bullied and more as if people were cheering for me to win. They were connecting with me, finally understanding that I had the energy to become the best and was showcasing wins in the work I was producing. One of the checks and balances came from the COO of Farkus Comm.

As I stumbled my way through the interview, I had the pleasure of talking with the company's COO, Anne, who took our interview down a path of favorite movies, which turned into a conversation about the greatness of *Office Space*. This was perfect for me, given *Lumino Magazine* had just completed its *Office Space* issue, and I had the fuel and celebrity stories to add value to our discussion. I was able to leverage some confidence and differentiation within the conversation. I was slowly building momentum.

As I left, I was handed a writing test. Clearly, they wanted to see if I was a good writer or a not-so-good writer who had had great editors.

After a few short days, the agency's president responded with an offer: $30,000 per year salary plus health care.

I responded, telling her that it would be tough to leave a job that was paying me $35,000 (and by $35,000, I meant $29,500) for a career shift, but I would think about it. As an increasingly confident twenty-four-year-old, I wanted to gain more market value for myself. I had gone from an "I'll take what I can get" attitude to a "pay me what I am worth" mentality. My momentum was building.

She replied and said she could go up to $32,000, but that was it.

I had a decision to make. It was time to take action. I went back to the *Northwest Herald* and told them that I had decided to make a jump. They asked if they could counter. I said, of course, but to stay, I wanted $40,000 per year, the ability to work from home a few days a week, to be a full-time features reporter, and to no longer report to my current boss. I was not overly fond of the way she failed to cultivate my drive and constantly dismissed my potential. In retrospect, those job bullying moments fueled me more and perhaps were important to the velocity equation at that point in my career and life.

I bet, as you reflect on your equation and examine your foundational stage—whether currently in it or stepping into momentum—that you will have had moments, fork-in-the-road type moments, where you had a scary decision to make. A decision that would lead to an unknown result. I made plenty of wrong decisions, but in reflection, this was a right one.

Even after telling folks at the *Northwest Herald* that I was going to go to the "dark side"—as PR is often referred to by journalists, especially by those who make the leap—they offered to keep me on to write my column. Say what!? I'd continue my weekly interview column, where I tried to fluster celebrities with my dumb questions. Continuing with the column would provide $100 per week in extra cash, add $5,200 to my salary, and give me enough confidence and momentum to jump.

I took action. I accepted the job at Farkus. Despite my experience in journalism, I was hired at entry level. During my first week on the job, the COO asked me what I hoped to accomplish. I said that I planned on being a vice president within the next two years. She laughed.

That laugh had two impacts on me. First, the laugh made me want to prove her wrong. Second, it gave me an incredible momentum speed burst to jump into my job and show her I was capable.

She gave me an opening, and I was ready to run with it.

With momentum, you need to capitalize on your openings. You need to turn those lemons into lemonade.

I hadn't had any true training in PR, yet I was motivated. When you are motivated, anything is possible. Change is possible.

Not knowing how to "pitch" the media, I picked up the phone and started dialing reporters with what I considered great stories. The one consistency in my pitches was that I identified a human-interest aspect. Brands don't sell brands; people do. Reporters seemed to like this approach, as I would have when I was on the other side.

I could quickly present the finish line and then help the reporter piece together the pathway to getting there. This mapping strategy of starting with the end in mind ended up sticking as a theme for me—even today. I like to solve problems starting with a potential answer and then figure out how I explain that pathway.

The first hit (media placement) I got was with an Emmy Award–winning TV reporter in Los Angeles. This seemed to impress the executives at Farkus, especially since I booked it on my second day without any formal training.

This small action was essential to my career momentum. My confidence was extremely high, and I was ready to roll. I knew anything was possible after that moment. It was a moment where I was able to use a component of foundation in the momentum stage.

That "anything is possible" moment is important. When have you had those? Whether with weight loss (losing two pounds yesterday) or business (setting up a conversation with a potential client), celebrating the little wins is important to building momentum.

At this particular stage in my career, momentum was heating up. In my first full month at Farkus, I booked a hundred interviews.

That was quite the feat, considering the average person booked about ten per month.

My boss was always appreciative and gave thanks for a job well done, but she was always very careful in feeding the ego, my cockiness. She was a good mentor in that she tried to keep my spirits high without overinflating my anything-is-possible attitude. Her appreciation propelled me. Praise and appreciation fuel momentum.

I have also learned this as a boss. If we focus on celebrating the small wins and saying thank you, authentically, for jobs well done, we have a shot at winning, motivating, and encouraging our teammates to have a mindset that anything is possible.

In this particular run of events, I am able to look back and see all parts of momentum working together (stronger sense of confidence + one inch of difference + action). You, too, should be able to reflect on previous sequences of events and see your own momentum equation at work.

With a hundred interviews booked, I had a platform to stand on (stronger sense of confidence). I had proof that I was not a start-up, entry-level employee. I was good—damn good—and I knew it.

My foundation was evolving into momentum, and with fresh confidence and the support of my boss, I now had negotiating power.

I took action and told my boss, the COO, that I was hired at a lower level than I should have been and would like a review at the three-month point. Fairly confident, sure, but the proof was in the pudding. She agreed that my performance was an exception to the rule and granted my request.

Armed with my success chart (one inch of difference), I negotiated, and at that review, they bumped my salary to $36,000 and agreed that if I continued on the path I was on, they would promote me at the six-month point. Now, as I sit in a different chair in my business life, this is certainly risky to the egos of those you work with. There is significant danger in the growing pains through momentum, not for the individual or the believer but for the employer. Promote or give raises too quickly and ego can motivate someone into their next job at a different company.

Luckily for Farkus, I was loyal. I just wanted to earn the positions ahead of mine and prove that I could be the most valuable hire they had ever made.

At my six-month point, they were true to their word and bumped me up two positions to an account manager. I continued down this path, leapfrogging my colleagues, even quickly becoming the manager of my best friend at the agency. That was a tough experience for him—and a lesson to be learned by me.

When I started at Farkus in February 2005, I was at the bottom of the totem pole. By the time I was ready to leave the company about three years later, I had moved my way up to a senior account manager, the third-highest position in their company.

As I entered the final parts of the momentum stage of my Farkus years, I felt very comfortable with clients, my staff, and my results. Brick walls were no problem. Clients threatening to leave were no problem. Tough media stories were no problem.

Whenever a client was on the edge of leaving, they would bring me in to solidify the relationship and jump-start the results. I had established clear key performance indicators full of rewards and consequences.

I fully bought into the belief that anything was possible.

CHAPTER 10

The First Real Vision

F ull of momentum—more confidence, one inch of difference, and action—I decided it was time to take my future to the next level. Halfway through 2007, I was given my first strike, a significant blow during my momentum stage.

As an owner of a company, it is your job to limit these strikes with future entrepreneurs. If you strike an entrepreneur too many times, they will want to strike back, and strikes are not negatives for entrepreneurs; they are fuel. I know that it is my job to catch the entrepreneur before they catch me—meaning, if I embrace their entrepreneurial spirit and work with it, they will be a huge asset to my organization.

Entrepreneurial spirit is not trainable. You are born with it. For me, while the entrepreneur was deep in my blood, so was loyalty. I wanted to give Farkus the opportunity to capture my entrepreneurial spirit and help the company.

I decided I wanted to be a partner in Farkus. I knew it wasn't as simple as me asking for equity and them granting it to me. With equity comes risk alongside reward. I understood this. I was ready, guns blazing, to come up with a great idea that could positively impact their business; add me to their financial reward model; bridge the foundation I had created in the past, including my digital content experience with *Lumino Magazine*; and create longevity for our relationship.

I went to the owner of my company and asked if I could set up a pitch. Reluctantly, he said he would listen, but it would be a long shot if anything happened.

I pitched him a concept of a franchise portal—a website full of franchise offerings—blended with a magazine (similar content planning as *Lumino Magazine* but focused on entrepreneurial success stories). This would blend my understanding of lead-generation tactics (very important to franchise brands) and the run I was having with *Lumino Magazine* (despite not figuring out the cash side). I called this idea Chize, a play on the word "franchise." I presented the owner with a business plan, a presentation, and a mock profit and loss statement.

I asked the owner of my company to lunch. I planned to pay. It was going to be my chance to earn my way into becoming a business partner and show him that I was going to take the next step of my life and career very seriously. My foundation had prepared me for my momentum and led me to this velocity moment. I was full of confidence and belief that anything was possible.

I presented my twenty-five-page business plan and projections. Seemingly puzzled by my presentation and request to be a part of his family business, he said he needed to think about it.

About a week later he came back and told me that he was about to invest in another franchise portal and wasn't interested in mine.

But that wasn't all. (I had prepared for the no/strike.) He said he wasn't interested in being my partner, period. Strike.

Flying in a perceived velocity stage, I crashed directly into the momentum brick wall. My insides twisted. I was hard rejected!

He then went on to say that I couldn't do it because of my non-compete, which in reality wouldn't have been upheld in court per Illinois and Georgia legal standards and was not actually a non-compete but rather a non-solicitation agreement. More on that later.

This was a strike. And a big one. My confidence was dealt a huge blow, but in a different way than when I was called fat.

This time, I looked down at my beaten self, thought for a minute, picked myself back up, and said, "Well, fuck him. I am great— and I am not finished here."

I quietly went back to the drawing board—not telling him that I was going to fight back. Over the next six months, I Jerry Maguire'd (my aha moment, where I could see crystal clear what my business idea was) a clear business plan. This time, when smacked on one cheek, I was ready to face the challenge head-on. I was destined, through all of the nos, to prove to him that I was his next great partner. I wanted to give him all I had. I wanted to provide him with exceptional value.

I was scheduled for another review, and this time I was financially motivated. I knew how much the other senior account managers made. (There were no secrets. They made more than me, even though I outperformed them in every aspect of the job—new business, client retention, staff retention, and results.) I was the youngest of the bunch, yet I had less client turnover and more clients, and I had brought on more clients than anyone else. I also created a management system that took people the business was considering firing and turned them around. They offered to bump me from $60,000 to $65,000. I said $70,000 would make me happy. The president said I was being greedy.

She called me greedy. That was a strike.

At this point, my morale was turning negative. I felt as though the company no longer had my back.

Even when the people who should believe in you don't, they should still believe in your ability to produce great work and not interfere with your path to success.

What they didn't understand was that I was fueling up. Each time they said no, I bottled it up and had more fuel to do great things with.

I decided I needed to go guns blazing this time to really show them I was in, their best teammate, and ready to impact their business in a big way. I turned my new business focus even bigger and recruited a billion-dollar company as a client by leveraging a relationship I had. That, too, wasn't good enough. They said I wouldn't get full commission because they would have come to Farkus anyway.

Surprisingly, I didn't consider this strike three.

At this point in 2007, the end of summer, I decided to give it one last try. I didn't want to compete; I wanted to become partners with the agency and those whom I respected so much and desired to be like.

Since my Chize business rejection, I had been testing out some theories on MySpace—a still popular social media tool at that point—and came up with an alternative solution. I could use social media to drive press, sales, and controlled buzz.

I secured a story in *Entrepreneur* magazine for a client, in which the reporter addressed the question of whether social media would be here to stay or if it was a fad. The conclusion was indecisive. It was an opportunity for our agency to prove the critics wrong and be the first agency to bridge PR, social, and business. This would position them ahead of all other agencies, as no one had defined the social agency yet.

The owners of Farkus were not on social media, and they certainly were not socially sophisticated enough to get it. I quietly tested one of my theories, giving clients a true value-add and me the data to prove that my theory worked.

Equipped with confidence, I went to work. I created a hundred-page business plan and asked the owner to lunch. He declined, but he said he would, reluctantly, listen to my idea.

I presented and waited for his calculated response.

He smiled.

"Social media is a fad," I can very clearly hear him say, even now.

It was strike three, but for him—not me—this time. He pushed me off the ledge and challenged me to jump into velocity—the creation of my own agency, the greatest midsize agency that ever existed.

My foundation + momentum was working, and I started to set

my sights on the next stage, velocity. Velocity was taking the foundation and momentum and executing on the vision.

Timing is everything when making the decision to act on the equation. For me, it was him rejecting me. I was just given an undisrupted path to do something pretty damn cool—create the first social agency that existed without him wanting to compete against me.

CONFIDENCE + ONE INCH OF DIFFERENCE + ACTION

In November of 2007, I went with a client, Wing Zone, to *The Big Idea with Donny Deutsch*, a show about big ideas on CNBC.

I had developed a great relationship and friendship with this client and debated about whether now was the right time to ask for guidance and if it was even an appropriate thing to do.

Without inquiring about my idea, Adam Scott, one of the cofounders, slapped a piece of paper on the table and said, "This is your business plan. Now is your time to jump out on your own." Matt Friedman, his cofounder, said, "We will be your first client." They believed in me so much they were willing to map out my path for me.

With your business or your personal future endeavor, it's now your turn to start planning for your turn at velocity. As you can see from the previous pages, each of my steps were ingredients for the future. And still, today, as I continue to improve and evolve my agency, I wonder what this will mean for whatever is next.

Everyone wishes to grow, and they all desire a path to success. When you take the leap at your vision—stepping up to the line to run the marathon, declaring you will no longer eat bread, or quitting your job and starting your business—you enter velocity.

PART 3

Velocity

On March 3, 2008, I walked into Farkus Comm with a simple letter, one that would forever pivot my career, life, and journey. It was an "introduction to velocity" letter, otherwise known as a resignation letter.

I was still accessing the bullying of my past but also the bullying of the present. The owner of Farkus's obtuseness, his dismissive attitude toward me, and the company's efforts to rein me in or hold me back contributed to this fuel.

My people was built from my parents and industry pros like Matt and Adam from Wing Zone who supported my mission.

My belief was built from me executing on parts of my vision while within Farkus.

With a vision to create No Limit Agency established, my confidence was created from my work and my ability to provide great service and results to my clients.

My one inch of difference came from my business plan to create an agency that challenged the norms established by the biggest agency in the category.

My action was in preparing for the moment—establishing a financial support system and deciding to move to Atlanta, where more franchisors were based than in any other US city.

For the resignation letter to work, the collective had to be added up. The equation had to be established.

For the first time in my life, the bullying of my past had changed from painful moments to truly being recognized as an ingredient of my confidence. I was no longer afraid of what I could be called. All that fear was bottled up for the chance to enter the velocity stage. I was prepared to jump off the ledge and start my own business.

Not once did I second-guess my decision to leave Farkus. Sure, I was nervous, but I was ready for the change and whatever would come next.

At the first chance, I walked into my boss's office and asked if I could talk with her for a moment. She said sure. I said I had some bad news. I was putting in my two weeks. She asked where I was going. I said that I couldn't tell her, but she would learn soon enough. She said she would have to go talk with Nelson and Regina. I understood.

I went back to my office and waited patiently for the next steps.

For me, my =happiness vision was the chance to own my own business that could cause a disruption, be successful, and make money. I wanted to shake up the old and replace it with the new. And, now, I had a vision to do it.

While I had already established my momentum, it wasn't until the moment I fully committed to quitting that I recognized that I could see velocity in front of me. Prior to that day, I had seen brick walls as obstacles, but something about that day was different. I began to see those brick walls as opportunities.

I had my foundation (fuel + people + belief).

I also had my momentum (confidence + one inch of difference + initial parts of action).

I also had a firm willingness to make a change, and my fears started to diminish.

And, now, I had my moment.

By now, you should have been thinking about your moment, the moment you can see velocity ahead. What will be the trigger that makes you take a risk at winning your vision? What do you think it will feel like, and what do you hope to accomplish? For me, my velocity moment in my life and my career was starting a business. In order to do so with an all-in mentality, I had to recognize what velocity meant.

When in momentum, the choice is yours. Do you charge forward and create something great, or do you not see velocity and get stuck in momentum—not accomplishing your ultimate goal and building upon that success?

You will know when you are stuck in momentum. Being stuck in momentum is when you are stuck at the edge of executing your vision.

Visions are a lot like diving boards. The first step off the diving board for the first time is the toughest step to take. Fear of the unknown overtakes our concept of what may happen next. The beauty of the diving board, however, is that the water below offers support.

I remember, as a nineteen-year-old fat kid, working for the Park District of Oak Park, desperately hoping the kids I coached in summer camp would consider me a hero, not just the fat guy. To achieve this "hero" status, I had to do something monumental—which in retrospect makes perfect sense for this analogy—jump off a diving board.

My vision was to jump off the third platform at the pool. It was three stories above the ground. I slowly stepped up the steep staircase. As I climbed past the first platform, which I had jumped off many times as a kid, my fear increased. I began to doubt I could execute on my vision to be a hero.

I climbed past the second platform, which I had jumped off a few times as a kid. I knew that the risk was increasing, but it felt somewhat familiar.

As I made my way up to the third platform, the third floor, I remembered climbing up the same ladder as a kid. Both times I'd opted to climb back down in shame, as laugher rose from below that the fat kid was unable to jump off the hero platform.

Friends—or "friends"—would joke that all the water would splash out of the pool if I jumped. Or that the wind would carry my fat ass past the pool and onto the cement, breaking the cement, not me. Or that because I was so fat, I would hit the bottom of the pool and break a bone.

Those became my perceived fears too. And they'd been created by my surroundings—my non-support system.

This time, as a nineteen-year-old, those bullying moments became fuel. My foundation had gotten stronger, and my fear had dwindled.

As I put my fear on the third platform, I waved below to the twenty or so kids waiting for me to show them that, yes, it was possible at my size to jump off the highest platform known and succeed.

I now had my people to accompany my fuel. I believed this would be the time.

With claps and cheers (my confidence), I walked to the edge ready to go (the one inch of difference in this execution of the vision), looked down for the thumbs-up from the lifeguard, took three steps backward, counted down, and jumped (action).

The next three or so seconds went fast as I plummeted to the water below. I sunk to the bottom, yes, but quickly swam my way to the top. As I emerged, I raised my hands in victory, hearing the celebration from my kids bobbing alongside the edge of the pool. I reached for the ladder, climbed up, and was celebrated with a massive amount of high fives. Those kids considered me a hero.

I had just taken another step into velocity by jumping off the diving board. My vision was in full motion, and the next time, I would do it even better.

Had I balked at jumping, the story would have been much different. I would have been back in momentum, understanding the equation but not being able to execute on my vision.

Your gut will let you know when you are ready to jump into velocity. Fear will be gone.

EXERCISE

For you, it's time to redefine your vision and put the velocity process to the test. Read my version first and then list yours.

Reinsert your headline: To create the greatest midsize communications agency that ever existed.

Define the ultimate win: Creating my own sustainable businesses so that I never have to work for someone else again.

On a scale of 1-10, how confident are you that you can accomplish the ultimate win? Nine.

Reinsert your headline:

Define the ultimate win:

On a scale of 1-10, how confident are you that you can accomplish the ultimate win?

CHAPTER 11

A Firm Willingness to Make a Change

By this point, you have (or should have) thought a lot about what you want to accomplish. Now comes the moment where you no longer teeter-totter on your idea. You jump. You commit fully to executing your vision. There is no turning back from the diving board.

Timing is different for everyone. For me, it took twenty-seven years to reach that much-desired velocity moment, a moment where my story's dots were connected. For you, perhaps it may take less time, or it may take more. Everyone has their own story. Everyone has their own velocity.

You have already experienced tastes of velocity at the tail end of momentum. You have, for sure, accomplished something great or something that made you or your people feel great. At this point, you are figuring out what your next move is and where you will get the energy from to complete your task.

Think about a moment in life that was challenging. Draw a line and connect it to a moment that felt great in whatever dream you were pursuing. How did that experience influence the possibility of momentum in your moment?

What does velocity look like? Is it money, fame, happiness? Now visualize how you feel, what you look like, and what that winning formula looks like. Hold on to that, as that will be important to planning for your winning moment.

When you reflect on your past, take a minute to enjoy the wins. If you are an entrepreneur working your way through the momentum stage—or someone still trying to find their way in their career, their life, their marriage, their business—reflecting on the stories of the past is an essential piece to finding your entrepreneurial or personal velocity. The past will fuel your future.

THINK AHEAD

In order to make a firm commitment to a change on your way to accomplishing important pieces of your vision, it is important to think ahead, even though you may struggle with the concept.

To help coach myself through foundational and momentum challenges, I think about me in the future talking to me today—or me today talking with me as I struggled through my teens. We will all have bad days—lots of them—but the reality is life goes on (even when ours doesn't). Thus, as you think about what's next for you, I challenge you to write a letter from your future self. What would you tell yourself today?

Before moving on with the book, write your letter. Let your future self be the person you are chasing. Address the following as you write the letter:

For me, this is what = happiness:

For me, this is what has fueled my growth:

For me, this is what could potentially make me fail:

For me, this is what I will accomplish:

EXERCISE

This is what I would write:

Hello my friend,

The pursuit of happiness can drive your life, and you are not wrong for pursuing it. In fact, you should. For the next twenty years, find your happy places. Not in money or wealth, but in life.

So, mid-thirties Nick Powills, let me tell you this: Life moves fast. In fact, in the blink of an eye, you'll probably be rewriting this from the seventy-five-year-old version of yourself. Scary, right? Maybe—but maybe not.

Life will only become scary if you don't live each moment to its fullest potential—if you let the little things distract you from your big picture, which is what = happiness.

You can find the fountain of satisfaction, and you will do so by constantly trying to improve yourself as a human being, in both your personal and business lives. Bad things happen to everyone, but the good ones can always manage to find more good than bad in any situation. Karma, I still believe, is alive and well.

In business, you have to battle your way to the top—not of the businesses you create, but of the industries you so desperately want to be a leader in. Take the International Franchise Association, for example. You have this great desire to influence and inspire change. Your desires are right, but your timing is wrong. Politics is certainly a piece of the puzzle, but so is time. Yes, you have been in the industry as long, if not longer, than those of your same age, but there are plenty of people who have been in it longer. Keep speaking up. Eventually it will be your turn to create change within the association.

Keep doing what you are doing. By building a publication that is by far the most socially shared publication in the industry, you are making waves—and more importantly, you are getting people to listen. You are helping lead change through your voice, writing, and editorial. Align your in-person business missions with your virtual voice and you will be able to impact more and more businesses—just as you know you can.

While your intentions with your team (coworkers) should always be in the right place, know that sometimes no matter what you do, how well you try to treat them, there will be certain ones who disappoint you. Don't let this change you. Don't let this stop you from trying to create a wonderful environment for them.

Never ever believe the hype, though. The second you settle is the second someone else takes away what you have built. Keep innovating. Keep thinking. Keep challenging the norm. By doing so, you will have a chance to create the greatest midsize agency by the time you are my age.

In your personal life, stay true to your foundation, your wife, your kids, your parents, and your siblings. Have their backs. Constantly tell them you love them. Always love them—even when your wishes and beliefs don't always align. That foundation is—and will always be—critical to your success in life.

Life goes fast. You are very in tune with this now, but you will be more in tune when you get to my age. Don't take the little wins for granted. Enjoy them. Find ways to enjoy the ride.

You will lose friends. You will lose clients. You will lose money. You will lose support. But you will never lose the love of others as long as you love them equally or more.

The next twenty years are going to be an amazing ride for you. Stop and smell the roses. Say thank you. Continue to try to be a better person. And then, as long as you gave it your best effort, you will feel as though you constantly find what = happiness each and every minute, hour, and day throughout that ride.

Hang in there. Good things happen to good people.

Sincerely,
Me at fifty-five

Before I could leave Farkus, I needed two plans: the plan to change and a future plan.

My office was right next door to Regina's, the cofounder of the agency and wife to Nelson. I heard Anne walk into her office. I couldn't make out any of their words, but I was certain they were discussing my exit.

I then heard a dial tone on speakerphone. They were calling Nelson, who was out of the office traveling. I could hear the tones and then a "Where the fuck is he going?" scream that is forever etched in my brain.

Clearly, the exit was not going to be easy.

The call ended abruptly, and Anne came back to my office.

"Nelson is traveling, not happy, and would like to discuss this with you when he returns this afternoon. It would be really helpful if you could tell us where you're going," she said.

"I'm sorry, I can't," I said.

The hardest part of that conversation was that Anne had been a solid mentor to me. She taught me a lot about PR and client management. Yet if I was going to make this significant change, I had to set aside our relationship in order to create the smoothest break.

Later that day, Nelson returned. He walked right past my office and into his.

Regina came to my office and asked me to come with her to talk with Nelson. What happened next ultimately turned into more fuel for me. Even when in momentum or velocity, you will still have moments that further strengthen your foundation.

I walked into his office, and he asked softly, "Where are you going?"

"I am sorry, Nelson. I can't tell you."

That statement set off a fuse. Equipped with his attorney on speakerphone, he said if I didn't tell him where I was going, he was going to sue me (for no other reason than to try scaring me into telling him where I was going).

"I am sorry," I said. "I can't tell you."

He then said he would make my life hell. More and more expletives came out. Yelling turned to screaming. I remained stone-faced.

I decided it was time to conclude the conversation. I reached in my pocket and handed him the business card of my attorney. I had retained an attorney as a backup strategy for any unforeseen legal challenges that presented themselves. While I was not violating any part of my commitment and agreement, in this country, people can sue for any reason they want. I wanted to be protected.

"You can talk with my attorney if you have questions," I said.

"You have a fucking attorney?" he screamed.

This conversation was over.

Shaking, I walked with Regina back to my office. I shut the door. I was uncomfortable. That was another rough day. I called my parents. They said they would meet me for dinner. I packed up and left.

I was bullied (threatened with a lawsuit) and humiliated (yelled at in front of my peers), yet this time around I felt some confidence. Having led twenty-two accounts at Farkus, I had been willing to write up a fantastic report on how they could handle and keep those accounts, how they could maintain my process, and how they could win with my media contacts. I was prepared to give them everything. But after being screamed at, I changed my mind.

While I was at dinner with my parents, my phone started blowing up with calls and voicemails from Nelson. He wanted to talk. I told my parents I was unwilling to have a discussion with him. I needed a night to think.

The next morning, I was feeling brave, and I decided to go back in. When I arrived, Regina came into my office. She started telling me what she expected me to do before I left.

"Hold on one second," I said. "I have some rules first."

"Rules?" she said.

"Yes, rules. I don't appreciate the way Nelson spoke at me yesterday. Therefore, Nelson is not allowed to speak with me at all. If he does, then I leave without finishing a report."

"You can't set rules," she quickly said back.

"I can. And now, if you talk down at me too, I will leave. Communication needs to come through Anne."

Regina left my office. Anne came in.

"I can't believe you did that," she said, with a half grin.

"I have given this company my all. I wanted to be here forever. I desired a partnership. That wasn't in the cards. I will leave the right way," I said.

The next two days I kept my door shut. I was on a mission to turn in the most complete report ever. I finished it at around three in the afternoon. that Wednesday, handed it to Anne, and was immediately asked to leave.

I was on my own, and I wasn't scared.

DEFINE WINNING

When creating No Limit Media Consulting in 2008, I decided to go all in. I had a firm willingness to make a change—a big change. For me, this meant quitting my steady job, breaking up with my girlfriend, and moving from Chicago to Atlanta in the first month of business. This was the start to me really winning at what I wanted to really win at—being a business owner.

My definition of winning will always be different from yours. But knowing that there is appreciation in all forms of effort toward winning should help for both your and my people in the foundation sense.

Don't let the world dictate what winning is to you. You should define it to the world—be open and honest about expectations. This way, winning collaboration is possible, and both sides can be happy.

When looking into your future, how will you define winning? Have you written it down, drawn a picture, or told a friend? You should. There is some truth to visualizing the pathway to success. I constantly think about how I will feel when I earn a particular win. Visualize that feeling of winning, and it may help you increase your desire to get there. Communicate the winning path to your mentors, as they too can help you visualize the path.

Winning starts with fully buying into your vision and the change required to make it happen. As you step into the execution, becoming fearless will lead you to being able to break through all brick walls that block your path.

CHAPTER 12

Fearlessness

When making the firm decision to make a change, you may experience some fear. You may be afraid of the unknown. Eventually, that fear will subside and be replaced with fearlessness. When you mix fearlessness with your firm willingness to make a change, you have the first part of the velocity equation solved. You will jump off the diving board with confidence that the landing will be OK.

Quitting a job is not easy; neither is deciding to do something great. But when you no longer fear that change will hurt you, you will be ready for any and all changes.

Looking at fear differently takes time and planning. For me, I took my two rejected business plans, merged them, and built my vision for No Limit prior to quitting Farkus. With an understanding of my foundation + momentum formula, I experienced a firm willingness to make a change. Then I walked away from Farkus. I jumped.

The decision I made to quit my job, at the age of twenty-seven, was built from years of planning, years of opportunities, and years of failures. It wasn't the bad experiences themselves that I relied on. It was my ability to learn from them and turn them into fuel.

To set up that moment, I had to rely on a lot—from being overweight, to being told no, to being told I wasn't good enough, to finding my entrepreneurial velocity. I had to rely on my foundation to find my momentum to create my velocity.

The day after my last day at Farkus was the first day of the velocity of my vision. I was an entrepreneur. I was on my own. Whatever happened next would be in my control.

Fearlessness doesn't come without its challenges. For me, there were plenty of challenges in the first few months after quitting Farkus and stepping into velocity with No Limit Media Consulting, including the following:

1. The day after I quit, someone busted out my car windows. Oddly, nothing was stolen. Fear that someone was sending a message certainly entered my mind but left just as fast. I was up for anything.

2. That same day, I got a call from a friend who said he had heard I had quit. He wanted to connect me with a potential client. I got on a call with the prospect, who said that if I jumped on a plane to New York, he would sign up as our first client. Looking at my bank account, which had

$10,000 in it, and knowing this last-minute flight would cost $1,000 created a moment of fear, but the fear went away immediately because I was willing to do whatever it took to be great.

3. That first client didn't pay his bills. In fact, when all was said and done, he stiffed me $10,000 in retainer fees. The fear of dealing with unfair clients could have set in, but it didn't. I just continued to hustle for the next client.

4. The second client I signed had me do a rush project to launch their new franchise in Philadelphia. I had all of the local media committed to coming to their launch event. The morning of the event, the VP of development called me and said I had to cancel all media. He wouldn't tell me why. I googled the name of the president and found out he'd been arrested because of connections to the mob. Clearly, I didn't try to collect the money they owed me.

5. Deciding to move to Atlanta was a big deal. I moved two months after starting the company and only had industry friends as my people there. I left the stable foundation to fully commit to my vision. Fear? Nope. I was confident that I was doing the right thing.

Fear can certainly be recognized in the velocity stage, but your interest in breaking through all brick walls that come in front of you overpowers it.

The thing about velocity is that the success of it is dictated by the person executing it.

Real velocity involves risk. It involves a firm willingness to make a change. My risk was leaving stability for a chance at something amazing. A different life. A life full of foundation + momentum = velocity.

In order to have fearlessness, you will need to—

Identify the risks of your move:

1.

2.

3.

4.

5.

Find the simplest solutions to the above risks:

1.

2.

3.

4.

5.

Decide the timing. When?

Determine how you will do it:

1.

2.

3.

4.

There are many things you cannot control, but one thing that you can control is your mood and your fear. Find a way to celebrate every waking moment so that you can smile on your way out of this crazy, crazy world.

INNOVATION

In business, there are things you can control. You can control change. You can control adaptation. You can control =happiness outcomes (more on that later).

Think of some of the greatest brands we have seen during our lifetime. Remember Blockbuster? RadioShack? What about Pan American Airways? They're gone. Do you think they had leadership in the velocity state? Oldsmobile? Gone. Amoco? Gone. Hummer? Gone. Saab? Gone. Same with these.

What do all of these iconic brands have in common? They were all once great, and now they are gone. This may be in part due to their failure to change or their failure to innovate, but more so, it's due to their failure to jump into velocity. Or, more importantly, their fear of change.

Fearlessness would have created adaptation. Fear created an unwillingness to change, to face the edge of the diving board head-on.

Think what would have happened had Blockbuster said they were going to compete against Redbox first and Netflix second. They might still be here today.

Fear of the leadership prevented a new path from being created.

While great ideas change, others die because of fear. Innovation can help you overcome fear. Think back to your vision. How will you become innovative when creating your conclusion? How will innovation intersect with your vision?

For me, it was going to be through Chize and social media— the two ideas my former employer clearly did not have interest in executing.

HOW DO YOU BECOME INNOVATIVE?

My advice is simply that I don't think there is a right way and a wrong way to become innovative. It's more about whatever works. I try to get my head away from the daily norm and into a place where I can think about problems and then the solutions. I think about the numbers, colors, furniture, and genius exercise to help me identify innovation.

I start with a whiteboard and a topic. Whether it's franchising, marketing, PR, digital, social media, or advertising, I need a starting point. Then I simply start brainstorming.

I don't think anyone is an absolute expert when it comes to marketing and communications. Sure, there are those of us who can come up with a million ideas on the fly, but many of those ideas would fall flat on their faces. In marketing, it's a lot of guessing and then celebrating when something works out and making excuses when something doesn't.

Innovation shouldn't come yearly; it should come daily. As leaders and marketers, we should try to make improvements every day. That constant battle to get better is what will ultimately win the rat race.

Whether a basketball player trying to make more free throws (unless you are Shaq) or a baseball player adjusting their swing—the best of the best in this world are those willing to listen to advice, read the data, and make quick changes. And when a company can have leadership focused on innovation with the willingness to adjust and change, the company and its people have a chance to win.

I can't guarantee the future, but I know that innovation will continue to be a priority for me as I fight to sustain velocity.

Each time I think about change, I jot down every thought that enters my brain. (You should see my scratch notes.) I try to weigh the positives and negatives and the potential wins and fallouts from my plan. Those on my leadership team who listen to the possibility of change are probably slightly stressed. They likely wonder how change would affect the business today. I wonder how change could help the business tomorrow.

When owning your own business, fearlessness also comes in the inability to quit your job. You are in. There is no quitting. When the going gets tough, you deal with it. You don't quit. This is a form of fearlessness.

At the end of the day, there is only one person who cannot quit No Limit Agency or 1851—that's me. Sure, that's a lot of pressure, but it's also a lot of fearlessness to constantly find ways to win more for our clients and for our team.

I don't like bad days or bad moments that challenge the fearlessness—and when I do experience one, I try to find ways to not be afraid of the moment and to find a positive pathway to the exit. Most of the time, it's my wife or my children that bring me back to =happiness. I need them to help return my mind to the right place and to make my fears diminish. We all need a positive support system in potentially scary moments. It helps us mitigate fear.

The reality of death can also teach us about fear and truths. The shortness of life teaches us that none of us are invincible. It teaches us that we should never take too much for granted. Spending our limited time in this world not appreciating the little things will only breed regret.

While the fear of death motivates me to live in the moment, it also motivates me to create building blocks each day. Am I setting up a continuation of velocity for the long term?

I am constantly thinking about what the world will look like ten years from today. I am not sure if this is an entrepreneurial mindset or limited to a select few, but I am so committed to winning (not just financially but mentally) that while riding this wave of momentum, I can't help but see this beautiful potential light at the end of the tunnel.

For those who live this day to day, it may not be easy and may cause some forms of fear. I wish I could make it easier for them today. My intentions are that any change I put in place today will impact them more and more as the days go by. I don't just want to win for me; I want to win for them. I want to help them find what = happiness in our business.

One important lesson I had to learn in business adjustments was to think about how to improve the model not just for those who are in the business today but also for those who will be in the business tomorrow. Structure and process must be the driving factor to finding the next right business equation. If I can nail down both structure and process, with myself and my leadership team, we will have a shot at becoming the greatest midsize agency that ever existed.

To win at velocity, clearly, you can't be afraid.

Great leaders are not afraid of change. In fact, they embrace it, especially when the consistency plan skews a little off track.

When bumps in the road occur, innovation, adaptation, and separation from the statement "because that's the way we have always done it" are so vital to long-term success of businesses and the vision of being the best in whatever category you represent. Not being afraid of change will help executors correct course. A firm willingness to change + fearlessness will help you continue to break through all brick walls and will motivate you to truly find what = happiness.

The collective will equal velocity.

CHAPTER 13

= Happiness

A close friend of mine once said to me, "I don't think you are ever going to be happy." I replied, "I am extremely happy in my personal life" and "Don't misconstrue my mission for being the greatest in business as unhappiness. I'm just never willing to settle."

That night, I thought about what he said. Was I lying to myself about my level of happiness in business, in life, in this velocity adventure? I sat at my kitchen table thinking about this late into the night. I concluded that he was wrong. Here's why.

This friend of mine lost his mother at a youngish age. I can't imagine how painful it is to no longer be able to talk to a parent because I have the tremendous fortune of still having both my parents. On that level, I cannot relate to him, and he can't relate to me.

Our foundations are different. Our momentums are different. Our velocities are different.

He had the experience of hitting *his* rock bottom. His worst day ever is arguably worse than my worst day ever. This means his understanding of sadness and loneliness is different from mine. It's not different in that mine is weaker or wrong; it's different in the fact that the fuel that powers each person's foundation is shaped differently.

Your =happiness is created by the experiences you go through in life. Everyone's is different, which means a broad evaluation of happiness, in my opinion, is false.

Happiness can be different in business and in life. I can leave a hectic day and replace it with a large smile when I get a greeting from my wife, a hug from my oldest son, and a giggle from the baby.

Happiness for me in the workplace comes alongside very high expectations. I know I expect the "hard to attain," but for me, that's the drive. Clearly, it's not the drive for everyone.

Happiness is the Zen moment when you feel happy. There doesn't exist a one-size-fits-all happiness equation because happiness is an individual experience.

What brings you happiness should be an important part of measuring the execution of your vision.

When reflecting on the start of No Limit and this pursuit of =happiness, I see many ups and downs—great hires, bad hires, great partners, bad partners, great clients, and bad clients. The one caveat that I have learned is that even when people are not great fits in business, they can still be good people, and it's up to you, as their leader, to find their =happiness, whether in your company or in another. Sometimes, it can be right person, wrong seat;

sometimes it is nice person, wrong company; and sometimes it's wrong person, wrong company.

On a mission to help my team define the right human situation (in, adjust, out), I often call meetings with the up-and-comers of the agency. My agenda is simple: try to gain a glimpse into their minds to try to define what "X" and "Y" is in the equation of =happiness for them. I try to determine what they need to continue to be happy at my company and how I can help provide this to them.

The reality, I tell them, is that they will have to work until they don't. Meaning, they will work at least until they either have the financial wealth to not have to or decide with a future partner that they don't have to work. We are all going to have to work for a while, so you might as well love it while you're doing it.

We have a fancy office, share amenities with the biggest agency in the world, have increased our average salary by 45 percent each of the last three years, and are constantly adding more and more talent to hopefully (fingers crossed) positively impact the stress levels. We are constantly challenging ourselves to figure out what else we can do to make this company better and be a part of the equation for =happiness.

What I learn from these short meetings is that each person has a different take on happiness. I see this on their faces and hear it in their voices. Many reflect on leadership and the tasks they are responsible for. A common theme for =happiness is team collaboration. Great, I can give them those things.

For CEOs, happiness is critical to our success as a business. I will continue to look at the numbers and KPIs, but if we can come to an understanding and agreement on what should be expected, then it's up to me to equip my leadership team with the tools to deliver =happiness.

I tell them that in the ideal scenario, no one would ever leave No Limit as long as I could give them the "X + Y = Happiness." (I know, it's unrealistic, but one can hope.) On the flipside, should they not find what = happiness, then they should be motivated to move on to their next step and find it through what is winning for them.

I find winning to be fairly simple. The difference between good and great is not that significant of a difference. That one inch of difference can be found in creating incredible moments through great service. In my business, I see success under the following pillars.

IT STARTS WITH SERVICE

If you want to make millions in your career—whether you own the business or not—start with a good service plan. For entrepreneurs, this means going above and beyond when it comes to customer service. There are certainly exceptions to the rule. For example, once you have customers who have indicated that they love you, you'll certainly have more leeway in the aftermath of your bad service. Case in point, I was flying back to Chicago from Atlanta after attending an industry conference. Shockingly (not), my Southwest flight was delayed—by three hours. I asked a Southwest staff member if it would be worth it for me to try to switch flights and if the delay was due to a mechanical issue. Without looking up, he said, "I don't know. You can do whatever you want." His comment was pure rudeness for a company "known" for great service. The problem with this situation was that something similar happened with the second team member I talked with.

If you don't take care of your customer, someone else will. Although I will continue to fly Southwest (because it's an awesome value), I write this aboard a flight to Miami on American Airlines. We will see if they can service better.

CREATE =HAPPINESS FOR YOUR CUSTOMERS

Once you service, it's time to do what you say you will do and create =happiness for your customers. The problem with that flight was that not only did Southwest not do what they said they would do (leave at a planned time), but they also gave me attitude for no reason. This is what will kill a business—especially if it becomes consistent. If you don't do what you say you will do, you will still win if you do everything you can in the calmest way possible to resolve it. At No Limit Agency, we always try to do what we say we are going to do. In fact, this principle has really morphed into our one major core value: Give a Shit. When you Give a Shit, you have the opportunity to make millions, because you won't let the little things get in the way of providing great service and results for the customers.

TAKE CARE OF YOUR PEOPLE

After you do what you say you will do, it's time to take care of your people. People are what will ultimately make you more money. Whether you are a senior leader who wants to move up the executive chain or you are an entrepreneur trying to scale your business, people are the secret ingredient to success. The quicker you realize this, the better chance you will have at being great. And if you treat your people right, they will Give a Shit, and they will treat your customers right in turn.

YOUR =HAPPINESS IS EQUALLY IMPORTANT

As a business owner, I feel that if you start with =happiness and then define winning, the process can start to take care of itself.

As an individual, I feel that =happiness comes from executing on all parts of the velocity equation.

Think about it. When you start looking at tough moments as fuel for your vision, you will become happier when dealing with bumps in the road.

When you have the right people in your corner, you will feel supported and loved. This will increase your happiness.

When you have belief, you will know you can accomplish great things. You will believe you can win.

When you have a stronger sense of confidence, you hold your head up higher. You will feel good with the steps you are taking in life.

When you have identified your one inch of difference, you will know you have something different to offer to this world, and that will make you feel great.

When you create action, you see that anything is possible.

With the mindset that life is short, we will want to achieve =happiness in the small moments and in our long-term approach to life.

I often think about the brevity of life and what will ultimately equal fulfillment in =happiness. It could be money. It could be success. It could be a successful marriage. It could be being a gold-star father. It could be a combination of all those things and many more.

Clearly define what = happiness. Go for that. Use that as your motivation for jumping off your ledge. Use that to define what = winning.

Is it financial rewards? Is it a pat on the back? Is it being the biggest? Is it being happy? Is it spending more time with your family? Is it moving up in your job?

Winning is ultimately up to your perception, and your perception is reality.

When you let the world dictate what your version of winning is, you lose. You can never meet the expectations of the world, only of yourself.

What does success ultimately look like? List it in two categories: business and life.

Business happiness looks like—

1.

2.

3.

4.

5.

EXERCISE

Continued

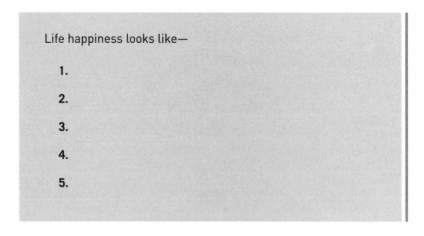

Life happiness looks like—

1.

2.

3.

4.

5.

Winning, for me, starts with happiness. I am on this roller-coaster hunt for happiness. I have written about it many times, but I still have yet to clearly define it in all categories of my life.

On December 3, 2008, nine months to the day of quitting Farkus, I was invited to the Roark Capital holiday party. Roark Capital is a big private equity firm that primarily holds franchise brands. Two significant events happened that night.

When I moved to Atlanta, I didn't know many people, so I decided to take up a hobby—coaching kids' basketball. My team wasn't so good, and we only won one game, against the other team from the same community center. On a positive note, my assistant coach was a partner at an accounting firm that represented franchise brands, and his son was on the team.

That night at the holiday party, I bumped into him. He was accompanied by a beautiful young lady. The lady was talking with a group of people I knew, so I inserted myself into the conversation. I introduced myself, but she didn't seem interested.

As the conversation with the group concluded, she started

exchanging business cards with the others. I saw this as my opportunity to get her card. I had fuel, people, and belief that I could earn a date with her.

She took my card, but she did not give one back.

The next day, I called one of the guys in that group and asked for her name and email. I said I was looking to hire an accountant (not the truth). He said her name was Sharon Kelly.

I looked this Sharon Kelly up on Facebook and messaged her saying it was nice to meet her the night before.

She replied, "Thanks."

I replied, "I hope you didn't drink too much and got home safely."

She replied, "I don't drink."

I replied, "Does that mean you want to get a coffee with me?"

She replied, "I am super busy [she was studying for the CPA test]. I can in February."

I replied, "That's great. I am busy until then too."

That won some points. We kept up the banter. She agreed to meet me for breakfast and coffee.

Today, her name is Sharon Powills. She is my beautiful wife.

The second event that happened that night was that it was the first time I'd seen Nelson, the CEO of Farkus, since leaving. He had flown in for the holiday party.

When walking out of the bathroom, our eyes locked. Neither of us said anything. Oddly, I didn't have any fear in the moment. I still felt pure happiness that I could and would not be bullied by him.

Everyone's happiness will be different. It will be unique to you. The most important factor of velocity will be what = happiness.

CHAPTER 14

Sustaining Velocity

Are you ready for the first day of the rest of your life? Are you ready for the moment when you sustain success in the execution of your vision?

Every day I think about sustaining my velocity. I reflect on my past, recognize my fuel, believe in my momentum, and trust in the velocity equation.

Part of sustaining velocity is understanding that it could end at any point. You could be bullied again. You could fail again. You could fall again. You could retreat off the ledge again. However, remembering that life is short can help guide you to pick up the pace of your decisions.

Sustaining entrepreneurial velocity will require an anything-is-possible attitude, a work-harder-than-everyone-else mindset, and a dream to accomplish something bigger.

These are characteristics that I try to live by at No Limit Agency as I continue the velocity stage of my vision.

As I write this in 2018, No Limit Agency is a thirty-five-person shop based in the Prudential Building in downtown Chicago. We relocated the business here in 2011 because we knew the Chicago market had more potential agency talent than Atlanta.

We also run a publications division, which houses 1851 (what ultimately came out of Chize). Both businesses have seen great success—including No Limit being a four-time finisher in the Inc. 5,000—and continue to sustain velocity and upward movement. This is my velocity.

YOUR VELOCITY IS YOUR STORY

Sustaining your velocity will be essential to building on greatness with more greatness. To maintain greatness, try to do the following:

- Sustain your belief, destroy your self-doubt.

- Give a Shit; care deeply about your accomplishments and use them as motivation.

- Deal with setbacks.

- Understand your limitations.

- Quickly recover from your mistakes.

- Be proactive.

• Manage relationships.

For many, sustaining velocity is all about growth. As a salesperson, if you did ten deals three years ago, fifteen two years ago, twenty last year, and then show pace for seventeen this year, disappointment will show its ugly head. Even though you have shown growth, the expectations of pessimistic leaders will not align with your results. You will have a little failure tag placed on you because, unfortunately, many in power focus mainly on results. It's hard to celebrate seventeen deals when you did twenty the year before, even if seventeen represents crazy monies in future earnings. It is simply not good enough because the path changed.

Sometimes winning is still losing for those who see results in black and white. This is why winning needs to be about more than financial growth.

In a life that is too short, it's sad that we are so dependent on increasing expectations forced by the fear of failure. This probably creates bumpy cultures and workaholics. Life and work would balance much better if results were looked at as a hundred-point process versus a final deal count and growth was simply that. One more unit is one more unit.

Part of maintaining your velocity—whether entrepreneurial or not—is understanding what success looks like for you. The other part is an understanding that it could end at any point.

But, of course, you never want any of these things to happen. So, you continue fighting and continue remembering that life is short. This can help guide you in picking up the pace of your decisions.

Remember, though, sustaining velocity doesn't have to fall into a singular approach. It can be customized to you. Sustaining velocity for you may be running your first half marathon and then running other races thereafter.

The chance at velocity starts with using foundation + momentum to dominate your vision. You are standing on the ledge. You have a plan to create something great. You are now faced with two decisions: Do you jump, or do you not?

If you are looking at a brick wall, you are not ready. If you are not ready, you still need to work through the foundation and momentum portions of the equation. And that's OK. Don't fret if you aren't there yet; just keep working through your own story until you arrive.

If you are looking through the brick wall, you are ready to go.

When staring at entrepreneurial velocity, you may choose to turn away from the beautiful view below. If you do, it's not a problem. But understand that the clock is ticking. If you want to live with no regrets from this point moving forward, then don't make excuses.

And when you are in velocity, keep building upon your foundation, momentum, and ultimately, your entrepreneurial velocity.

If you've had tremendous sales periods, but you got stuck, and comp sales aren't what they were before, you might start feeling as if the sky is falling. You'll have to adapt and try to jump-start sales velocity through other innovation. You'll need to look through the brick wall and understand that the brick wall won't be able to stop you.

Don't forget, you can take an entrepreneurial approach to your personal life or career. Velocity comes from applying entrepreneurial attitude and techniques to your life, but it's the same equation for both:

FOUNDATION (FUEL + PEOPLE + BELIEF) + MOMENTUM (STRONGER SENSE OF CONFIDENCE + ONE INCH OF DIFFERENCE + ACTION) = VELOCITY [(A FIRM WILLINGNESS TO MAKE A CHANGE + FEARLESSNESS) + =HAPPINESS]

My formula for losing weight:

Foundation (bullying + support system + believing I could beat my eating habits) + momentum (looking in the mirror and seeing something different + deciding that I was going to walk to dinner versus taking an Uber + cutting bread from my diet) = velocity (continuing to diet long term + running five miles per day + losing weight and feeling great).

You see, the equation can work in multiple ways.

Once the growth vision is set, it's hard to step away or stop building on your velocity. Even when there are brick walls, you will continue to fight through.

How do you see the brick walls you will eventually break through?

Here are two examples of brick walls I've broken through.

PERSONAL BRICK WALL

When I graduated college, I weighed 270 pounds. Though I played basketball three times a week, I was considered unhealthy. Even though I had tried Weight Watchers going into my senior year of college, I didn't sustain it. I was thrown back into figuring out momentum versus velocity.

I decided I would try again, and this time was going to be

different. I committed to Weight Watchers again in 2003 and lost 40 pounds. I remained at 230 pounds until right after I got married. This is when I decided to break through the brick wall and really execute on my vision to be healthy.

I eliminated cream from my diet. Then I eliminated soda. At that point, I was ready to turn from momentum to velocity, and I eliminated bread. Today, I weigh 210 pounds.

As someone who has battled weight issues his entire life, brick walls come up every day—every time I have to say no to bread, pizza, and beer. I listen to my inner self saying I can do it, and I remind myself of how many times I have said no and how hard I have had to work to get to this point. There is no quitting the weight battle.

BUSINESS BRICK WALL

Listening is a powerful tool for breaking through brick walls. Don't overlook the knowledge you can gain by opening your ears and being open to constructive criticism.

In an effort to find more transparency and create expectations of future brick walls, at No Limit Agency, we put a grading system in place. It works great, as we are able to understand how our clients are feeling about strategy, service, relationship, and results, as well as how we can get better. This has been a process, and I have learned a lot from it.

I put this strategy in place not because I love hearing what we are doing wrong. I did it to figure out what we needed to do to get better and when we needed to get better by.

I want our clients to always be happy with our service, relationship, strategy, and results. I want them singing their praises for NLA from the rooftops. I also want to fix things before they get too far broken. Here's what I learn from listening in business while sustaining our velocity.

There are norms in client turnover in the agency world. It is almost expected. I wanted our agency to challenge this. We know that if we don't take care of our client, someone else will. We need to hold this sacred as an agency, really listen to what our clients are saying, and try to put solutions in place to preserve the relationship for as long as possible.

Our grading periods are quarterly. We ask for our contacts to grade us on a scale of 1-10 in strategy, service, relationship, and results. During one of our grading sessions, I learned some key lessons that I feel can be impactful to any business.

Relationships can be shaken—work to create consistency. Even when you think everything is going great, sometimes there are things you could be doing differently and better, especially when it comes to the expectations of the client. Even if your results have climbed year over year, sometimes that's not enough. This is why we evaluate other categories in addition to results to try to gain insight into our overall performance. Don't ever let your guard down when it comes to improving in strategy, service, and relationships as they are as important as results. Know that the moods of a business can create memory loss from your last big win. Keep the wins consistent.

It's not one size fits all. Some clients love grades. Some hate them. Some like them every six months. Some like them every quarter. We need to adapt our systems to best fit those we are seeking transparency from. This way it will be mutually beneficial. The end goal of the grades is for us to find ways to improve—not to create frustration for those from whom we seek feedback.

Constantly set expectations. Our agency has fully evolved from a PR/social media agency to a full-service agency. We handle creative, web development, media planning, marketing strategy, and development strategy in house. When your services expand, sometimes the clients who engaged you for one service expect wins in the others. Absolutely find ways to give value adds, but ensure the relationship grows on both sides. Be transparent with expectations. Talk about them frequently to ensure everyone is always on the same page.

Think every month is your last month. When NLA looks at campaigns, we do so as if they are building blocks—not final products. This way, each campaign should build on the last. From a media standpoint, all our clients are getting better press this year than they did in the past. Create landmarks and fight to surpass them each month and quarter. If you build the momentum, you own that momentum.

If your win falls in the woods, no one will hear it. We are constantly working on strengthening the transparency in the way we deliver our results to our clients. Their perception will always be the reality. We need to make sure they are always equipped with the right data on what we have accomplished. They might not be the ones who think the results are dipping—it could be someone else in the leadership chain. If you equip them with basic result data, they will be equipped with something they can forward. If you win and no one knows it, it isn't a win.

I was initially afraid to hear from clients that they were unhappy with an aspect of what we were doing. No one likes to hear bad news (unless, of course, you are an avid viewer of the five o'clock news), nor do we want to hear that a client could potentially be interested in exploring other opportunities.

Although that statement can cause anxiety and make brick walls appear, it also can provide something beautiful—knowledge and the ability to break through.

Knowledge is power. Knowing what a client is frustrated about offers an opportunity to fix it and make the relationship a million times better. Knowing what your significant other is frustrated with is an opportunity, as is listening to your inner self and identifying your personal frustration moments on your adventure to growing into a better, happier person.

In the PR world, reasons a client becomes frustrated aren't always black and white. Sometimes they're very gray, such as, "I just don't think we are getting enough press." That statement leaves little as far as tangible solutions, and sometimes when you bust your butt to get those extra "results," they are not good enough. However, this can help guide you to at least attempting a solution through agreed-upon expectations.

The same grading is going on right now for consumer brands; it's just a matter of whether or not they're listening. The beauty of consumer brands is that, through review sites and social media platforms, you can hear what your customers, clients, or guests are saying about you. Does that pizza you labeled the greatest thing ever fail to meet expectations because you priced it too high for what the customer got? Did your manager fail to use the words "I'm sorry" when a customer was given the wrong meal? Did your team forget to yell, "Welcome to Moe's"? All of this information sits within the pages of the internet because bad service is often talked about on Yelp!, Glassdoor, TripAdvisor, and so on, and it can help you find answers to service challenges you may have.

In business, service seems to trump everything, and the quickest pathway to improving your service is by listening.

At No Limit Agency, we strive to provide better service, relationships, results, and strategy than any other agency in the world. Perhaps it's a lofty goal, but by listening to our clients' needs, wants, and frustrations, we are able to make adjustments to better serve.

We also can see some indicators of what makes a great business in our listening. We have learned to—

- **Be obsessive about values**. At No Limit Agency, admittedly, we have struggled a bit with being obsessive about our values—not necessarily in practice, but in theory. The CEO of Toppers Pizza, Scott Gittrich, has nailed this, in my opinion. Along with his team, he developed core values for his brand that his staff seem to live each and every day. Live, not work. He has built an army of corporate staff, franchisees, and store-level employees who follow the company values, and when they don't, the process naturally removes them from the ride.

At No Limit Agency, we tried defining the values of the company only to have them turn into a chore versus an anthem. In talking with my team, we seemingly landed on something that could work for us: Give a Shit. That's what we do at No Limit; we just haven't defined it. I agree that to be a winning organization for a long time, you must be obsessive about values, but they cannot be forced. Don't create core values for the sake of creating core values. That's where we went wrong. Let the values be created by the culture, and be willing to adjust to changing times. Be obsessive about finding the path, not obsessive about forcing the definition.

- **Be obsessive about reputation.** This is something I believe we got right from day one—and I believe it is something that starts at the top. Part of the obsession with reputation could have been created from my own insecurities growing up as the fat kid, in that I have a great fear of disappointing others for fear that I will only get one chance to get it right. A lot of reputation is integrity—doing the right thing when no one is looking. We have been good at that. It's also transparency and doing what you say you are going to do. When you make a mistake, have the willingness to say you're sorry and make it right. Be willing to listen to criticism and learn from it. The importance of reputation is different for everyone, but for us, if we are going to be considered great long after I am gone, then keeping a disruptive approach to results, relationship, service, and strategy will be essential to us winning.

- **Be obsessive about promoting from within.** I wish we were better at this. If you have read my previous columns on culture—getting it right with your team, knowing that people power business—then you understand that I am obsessive about getting this right. It has just been a little slower for us to be great at it. Obsessive, yes; great, not yet. Promoting from within starts with hiring right. When our VP Lauren Moorman joined our agency, she placed a lot of focus on getting it right with the hire versus my approach of hiring people who had "sunshine" and "potential." This has slowed down our process a bit but has hopefully set a new path so that we will be able to hire better in the future.

We are taking the right steps to potentially have a business or businesses that are built to last and that are full of velocity, but we have a lot more work to do. I wonder if those businesses that have been around for a hundred years are still obsessive about the above categories. For me as a leader and us as a company, I believe that focusing on the above three will help create an umbrella or guidelines for what we need to pay attention to as a leadership team in order to see what makes our company better.

This listening doesn't just stop with our clients; it also extends to our team. If we understand how we can make our environment better for our team, we'll continue to find, keep, and reward great people. With great people, providing better service, relationships, results, and strategy will be easier.

Ever since that initial No Limit Media Consulting business plan, I have been highly focused on the power of longevity, especially as it relates to relationships. While partly naïve, I have this vision of only working with brands and people who desire a long-term relationship, not a short-term solution.

This vision is not easy to attain. Just like every other business, we still lose customers, even when we feel we did everything right, because frankly, it just wasn't a match.

After initially putting in the grading structure at our agency to try to gain insight into what was working and what was not, I saw an incredible hole in our grading system in that we were asking for relationship, service, and results but not clearly listening to the opportunity for solution that the collective feedback provided us: the initial and ongoing strategy. Without strategy all of those categories wouldn't give us the tools to make things great for our clients.

Change was not only OK but also needed to achieve more transparency and maintain the momentum we were building.

I learned that strategy was not just in the positioning of a brand, a story, a product, or a growth plan—it was also in the strategy of leading relationship, service, and results.

Within my discovery, even when we, as an agency, were delivering higher quality in each of the initial three categories, we were still missing the value of the rewrite at the grading points. We were asking them to grade us but not asking us to have a clean slate to start fresh and earn a better score and break through client brick walls.

Many of us are afraid to hear that feedback, but fundamentally and foundationally, feedback, stopgaps, and hard resets can be a simple solution to continuing a relationship. Listening has helped us break through the walls.

Today, every time a brick wall comes up, I feel confident that I will see the other side. This occurs in my weight battles and the building of my businesses.

You will start to see this too. You will see that brick walls are simply temporary obstacles. When you see them that way, you will be fully entrenched in the sustaining of velocity.

It's Time for You to Jump

Stop living the life you don't want to live. Start living the life you deserve. Even if the riches and fame you dream about seem impossible, start taking steps toward whatever your happy place is. Do it with ambition, with your dreams wide open, and with no regrets.

FOUNDATION + MOMENTUM = VELOCITY

In elementary school I was teased for being fat. Without a foundation this moment was taken as simply a critique without a vision.

With a vision and an understanding of momentum, this moment and other moments started to change.

In high school, I was told I wasn't a good enough writer to make the student newspaper. Looks as though I found a way to win that war.

In college, I was the only editor-in-chief of the student newspaper to not have an advisor from the journalism department because they said I was being too creative with my ideas. Look where I am today.

If you look at those experiences in detail in a half-empty way, those would be considered failures. However, I used them as my fuel to continue fighting for solutions. It's all in the way you look at the glass.

As you stare off your ledge, think about what you see. What vision does that ledge represent and what is the worst thing that could happen if you take a risk? My advice is that if jumping off will help you inch toward what could potentially = happiness, then what are you waiting for?

Are you afraid of making a mistake? If so, why? Throughout my life, I have embraced mistakes, as long as they are followed with a determination to get better—to continue fighting for success. This is breaking through brick walls. Problems with solutions. You cannot train work ethic, commitment, and loyalty, but you can train new methods, processes, and systems to help ensure that same mistake isn't made in the future. As long as the right attitude is accompanied by the mistake, greatness can still happen—and brick walls are just temporary issues.

You have a story. Now piece it together in the equation.

Crush your vision.

Revisit:

What is your headline?

Plan

What is your plan?

What are your points of differentiation?

What is your pathway to profits?

People

Who will be your influencers?

How will they help drive your profits?

Who will be your stars?

How will you keep them?

Places

Where will you market?

How will you market?

How will you tell your story?

Projected Profit

How are you going to make money or achieve personal happiness profit?

How much do you project to make?

Continued

How much do you need to make to be happy?

Type this into a single-page document, print it out, and use it as your blueprint for doing something awesome. Use it as your vision bible. Use it as your motivation. Use it to do something that leads you to =happiness.

Today I have gained entrepreneurial velocity in my business and personal life.

In business, I am confident that we have built a form of velocity. We work with one hundred brands. We occupy an office in one of Chicago's most signature buildings. We have an incredible team. We are impacting businesses in many different ways. We are creating new ideas and proudly jumping off the ledge and taking a swing at something else that could be great.

My personal side, while a constant journey, also feels great. I struggle daily with the idea of leaving behind the fat kid. In fact, every single time I look in the mirror, I see fat Nick staring back. This statement isn't meant to make you feel bad for me but for you to know that there will be parts of your foundation that you may never escape. Today I embrace those.

I embrace what I see in the mirror. I don't love what I see, but I embrace that it's been a part of my journey, of my story. It helps me try to eat healthier—leave the bagels be and the cream out of my coffee. Try is all anyone should ask anyone to do.

While internally I am still the fat kid, I have plenty to be happy about, including a wonderful wife, two great children, and a vision to remain healthy. Life is good. =Happiness is present.

Velocity is not guaranteed to work equally across all parts of your life, but the fundamentals of the equation are a good starting point to leading you to velocity.

To get to velocity, you will need foundation + momentum.

FOUNDATION = FUEL + PEOPLE + BELIEF

MOMENTUM = CONFIDENCE + ONE INCH OF DIFFERENCE + ACTION

Once in velocity, you will need a new equation to create sustainability.

SUSTAINED VELOCITY = A FIRM WILLINGNESS TO MAKE A CHANGE + FEARLESSNESS + =HAPPINESS

You will never forget the first day of feeling entrepreneurial velocity. The day I packed up my car to drive to my new city of Atlanta was the first day I was fearless. I was no longer fat. I was no longer a failure. I had velocity.

After your first day of fearlessness, I am confident you will continue to create wonderful success. And if you are living velocity correctly, you will find what = happiness for you. Life is short; find your happiness.

Anything is possible with a dream and the drive to accomplish it.

Momentum + foundation = velocity.

And =happiness is the goal.

For me, I am happy.

ABOUT THE AUTHOR

NICK POWILLS, CFE, founded No Limit Agency in 2008 and serves as chief brand strategist for the Chicago-based firm.

No Limit is a full-service communications agency that establishes and elevates brands by bridging public relations, social media, marketing, advertising, digital, and a lot of creativity to best strategize well-rounded and successful campaigns for more than a hundred global franchise brands. By presenting visionary ideas and building real relationships, No Limit is able to create effective media branding strategies to help companies grow.

Nick currently leads a staff of writers, media strategists, designers, social media experts, and digital producers in an office think tank where brands are humanized for strong, compelling media stories.

Powills also founded 1851 Franchise and estatenvy, two content marketing publications and platforms.

Prior to starting No Limit at the age of twenty-seven, Nick spent three years working at a PR agency, where he mastered the art of building rapport with media outlets and creating newsworthy pitches for earned media placements. He holds a bachelor's degree in journalism from Drake University in Iowa.